National Urbanization Policy in Developing Countries

A World Bank Research Publication

National Urbanization Policy
in Developing Countries

Bertrand Renaud

PUBLISHED FOR THE WORLD BANK
Oxford University Press

Oxford University Press

NEW YORK OXFORD LONDON GLASGOW
TORONTO MELBOURNE WELLINGTON HONG KONG
TOKYO KUALA LUMPUR SINGAPORE JAKARTA
DELHI BOMBAY CALCUTTA MADRAS KARACHI
NAIROBI DAR ES SALAAM CAPE TOWN

Library of Congress Cataloging in Publication Data

Renaud, Bertrand, 1939-
    National urbanization policy in developing countries.

    Includes index.
    1. Underdeveloped areas—City planning.
    2. Underdeveloped areas—Urbanization.   I. Title.
    HT169.5.R45   307. 7'6'091724   81-3999
    ISBN 0-19-520264-3   AACR2
    ISBN 0-19-520265-1 (pbk.)

Foreword

This book was originally written as a background study for the *World Development Report, 1979*, the second of a series of annual reports produced by the World Bank's economic staff. Each year the best of these studies are separately published for the use of scholars and practitioners in specific fields. The present work is one of three monographs dealing with problems of industrialization and urban development, the main themes of the 1979 report.

The need for active urbanization policies is greater for developing countries than it was in the past for economies that are now developed. Population is growing faster, rates of economic growth are higher, and the role of government is more pervasive in developing countries today. National urbanization policies have three goals: to correct the undesirable spatial effects of national economic policies; to make internal management of cities more efficient; and to increase economic efficiency and socioeconomic integration by eliminating the barriers to resource mobility and the diffusion of innovations.

Renaud shows why progress in formulating national urbanization policies requires coordination among these three goals, while uncoordinated policies have often worked at cross-purposes. He stresses that decentralization is not a substitute for the more efficient and more equitable use of resources within cities, particularly in large urban centers.

As do other World Bank research studies, Renaud takes a broad comparative view of his subject. His policy recommendations are soundly based in economic theory, but supported as well by a wealth of empirical illustrations drawn from the Bank's operational work.

Hollis B. Chenery
Vice President
Development Policy
World Bank

Acknowledgment

The author wishes to acknowledge the help and advice received from friends and colleagues in the preparation of this book, which owes its origin to the background work done for the *World Development Report, 1979.* Joel Bergsmann, Michael Cohen, Anthony Churchill, John English, Douglas Keare, and Johannes Linn have read earlier versions of the manuscript. Special thanks are due to William Dillinger who organized an economic and urban data file for 124 countries. Aeran Lee provided assistance for the collection of demographic data. Hansa Butani, Anita Economides, Mary-Anne Heraud, and Gladys Tivel shared the task of typing the manuscript in its various forms. Jane Carroll made many helpful editorial suggestions for the preparation of the final manuscript, which owes much to her skills. Raphael Blow prepared the figures; Harry Einhorn read and corrected proof; Ralph Ward and James Silvan compiled the index; and Brian J. Svikhart supervised production of the book.

Contents

Foreword   *v*

Acknowledgment   *vi*

List of figures   *ix*

List of tables   *x*

1. Introduction   *3*

   The Need for National Urbanization Policy   5
   The Formulation of Appropriate Policy   7
   Outline of the Study   10

2. World Urbanization: A Simple Typology for National Urbanization
      Strategies   *12*

   Worldwide Trends   13
   Factors Affecting National Spatial Development   36
   A Typology of Countries for National Urbanization Strategies   38

3. Determinants of the Growth of Urban Systems   *54*

   Urban Systems, City Size, and the Transmission
   * of Economic Growth   55*
   Role of Transport in Shaping Patterns of Settlements   67
   Role of Industrialization in the Concentration of Population   73
   Migration   87
   Rural-Urban Interaction and Growth Linkages   91
   Distribution of Rural Landholdings and Settlements Patterns   93

4. Current Status of National Urbanization Policy   *96*

   Weakness of Policy in Developing Countries   96
   Unintended Spatial Effects of National Economic Policy   101
   Problems of Large Urban Concentrations   107
   Regional Inequalities, Dualism, and Spatial Policy   116

5. Appropriate National Urbanization Strategies   *129*

   Basic Considerations   *129*
   Policy Measures   *131*
   Dominant Policy Issues in Various Countries   *133*

Appendix A. National Urbanization Policy in Latin America   *141*

   Urbanization and Spatial Development   *146*
   Regional Policies   *149*
   Country Scale and the Choice of Strategy: State Policy in São Paulo,
      Brazil   *151*

Appendix B. Urbanization in Large Centrally Planned Economies: The Soviet
      Union and China   *156*

Appendix C. Problems with New Towns: Some Illustrations   *161*

Appendix D. Comparative Urbanization Data   *163*

Index   *176*

Figures

1. Level of Urbanization and per Capita GNP   *18*
2. Country Groupings Used for Demographic Analysis by
   the U.N. Population Division, 1975   *20*
3. Level of Urbanization in Thirty-three Countries and Regions   *23*
4. Indicator of Level of Services in the Republic of Korea by City
   or Group of Cities, 1968-70   *85*
5. Relation between Primacy and per Capita GNP   *109*
6. National Growth and Regional Income Disparities in the Republic
   of Korea, 1963-74   *122*
A-1. Urban Concentration in Cities of More than 250,000
   in Latin America   *143*

Tables

1. Average Annual Rates of Increase in Rural, Urban, and Total World Population   14

2. Tempo of Urbanization between 1950 and 1970 for All Countries with a Population Greater than 15 Million in 1950   28

3. Share of Net Migration in Urban Growth, 1970-75   30

4. Percentage Share of Total Urban Population by Each Size Class of Large Cities   32

5. Size Distribution of Cities in Developed and Developing Countries, 1950-2000   33

6. Degree of Urban Concentration Ranked by the Primacy Index   35

7. Country Typology for National Urbanization Policy   40

8. India: Distribution of Urban Population by Size of Towns   44

9. India: Percentage Distribution of Urban Population for Cities of More than 100,000   45

10. Contrast between Expanding and Mature Urbanization   58

11. Occupational Structure of Selected Capital Cities   74

12. Manufacturing Firm Size and Employment Distribution: Comparison of Bogotá and Cali with U.S. Cities   76

13. Opening, Closing, and Relocation Rates of Firms in Bogotá, Cali, and U.S. Cities   78

14. Migration and City Size in Columbia, 1951-73   90

15. Regional Disparities Based on Gross Regional Product   118

16. Policy Measures for National Urbanization Strategies   134

B-1. Growth of Cities of More than 1 Million in the Soviet Union   157

B-2. Growth of Cities of More than 1 Million in the People's Republic of China   159

D-1. Urban-Rural Growth Differential, 1950-70   163

D-2. Percentage Share of Net Migration in the Growth of the Urban Sector, 1970-75   165

D-3. Urban and Total Population Growth Rates, 1970-75, Ranked according to per Capita GNP   167

D-4. Four-city Primacy Index for Selected Countries, 1976   170

D-5. Indicators for the Typology of Economies   171

National Urbanization Policy
in Developing Countries

1

Introduction

Most developing countries showed no interest in spatial matters in the 1960s, but the relentless growth of the national populations and the tendency for people to concentrate in larger and larger cities have generated much more concern for the patterns of human settlements. Given the much lower level of income and education of many of these urban populations, there is a definite sense that some capital cities are entering uncharted waters and reaching population levels new to urban policymaking. This concern is certainly not relieved by the recent wave of dissatisfaction with large cities—their congestion, pollution, deteriorating amenities, and declining social cohesion—so frequently voiced in Western countries. What is emerging is the realization that the spatial distribution of socioeconomic activities cannot be dissociated and treated independently from the broader issues of national economic, social, and political development.

Because of the popular concern with the need for decentralization, the problems of rural-urban balance, and regional inequalities, decisionmakers appear to be more willing to integrate spatial considerations into their national policy schemes. Despite political urgency, however, the selection of objectives, their validity, and the coordination of various policy instruments remain a new field of operation for national planners. The seemingly well-focused query "Is it possible to decentralize the population away from the capital region?" also raises questions about the sources of urban growth and the value of various policies designed to affect patterns of population settlements.

The questions raised in this book are: What are appropriate objectives for a national strategy to shift patterns of urban growth? Can a national urbanization strategy operate separately from other social and economic policies? Are there tradeoffs between a greater dispersion of economic activities among various regions and the rate of growth of the national economy? What kind of actions could or should be considered by a country to moderate or even limit the growth of the capital region? To what extent is it possible to channel economic activities through selected urban settlements? To what extent does the growth of new urban centers in developing countries differ from the experience with new towns in advanced economies? What is the relation between a city and its hinterland, and how do the rural and the urban sectors interact? Thus, a national urbanization strategy is not limited to solving the problems of population and economic concentration in the capital region. This is a frequent point of departure for national spatial planning efforts in developing countries, but in fact an urbanization strategy can be formulated even without a strong concentration of population at the political and economic center of a country.

An explanation is in order here to justify my extensive use of the expressions "national urbanization strategy" or "national urbanization policies." Many other terms have been used in various countries and by various professions (urban planners, political scientists, sociologists, geographers, or economists), such as "population distribution policy," "national urban growth strategy," "regional policy," or "community development policy."[1] Some of these expressions are limiting because they seem to exclude other considerations which should be legitimate concerns of national planners. Also, the use of the word "urban" in a developing country context often leads to opposing it to the term "rural." It is easy to move from there to the unwarranted and counterproductive assumption that an "urban" policy must be "anti-rural" or at least damaging to rural interests; it would be a very unfortunate point of departure for policy formulation because rural and urban areas can interact very positively. Seeing rural-urban policies as a zero-sum game is a rather myopic perception, particularly in middle-income countries. In practice, when formulating its strategy, a country will typically choose the phrase most apt to receive wide acceptance and to mobilize public opinion, given its particular circumstances.

---

1. Bureaucracies and large-scale organizations being what they are, related policy assignments end up in rather inappropriate places on the basis of such labels.

The Need for National Urbanization Policy

A national urbanization policy is especially important for
developing countries because the location of new economic activities and the movement of population affect the efficiency of
their national economies and the stability of their political systems. This book reviews the determinants of urbanization and of
the spatial concentration of people and industry as a country
grows and develops. It discusses dominant policy issues for various
countries grouped into six broad categories: very small countries
(in area or population), countries with limited domestic markets,
large low-income countries, middle-income countries, advanced
market economies, and centrally planned economies.

The core argument here is that all countries are better off with
a national urbanization strategy that is the outcome of a careful
national debate about economic, political, social, and cultural
goals. Decentralization is not always the issue. Quite a few countries do not need to work actively at decentralizing economic
activities from the main urban region. Their level of development
makes it not yet an issue or they do not seem to be suffering from
excessive urban concentration. In other countries, however, the
spatial effects of current national policies and government practices are never considered in spite of their great influence on patterns of urbanization. Whether these policies systematically
accentuate the tendency toward urban concentration should be
a matter of public concern, and the realism of various urban expectations should be reviewed carefully.

For several essential reasons the need for a national urbanization strategy is much stronger among developing countries than it
ever was in the economies that developed earlier. The rate of
urbanization of developing countries is much faster than that
experienced historically by the developed countries. By the year
2000 the entire world population will be more than 50 percent
urbanized. In 1900 only the most industrialized country, Great
Britain, had reached that level; even the United States did not
reach that level until 1920. This very rapid rate of urbanization
applies to populations that are still growing at rates that are often
two or three times the rates experienced by the advanced economies. Between 1970 and 2000, the world urban population is

expected to grow from 1.3 billion to 3.3 billion.[2] That is to say, the urban population alone at that time will be equal to the total world population of 1965. The rate of growth of developing economies is also very high by historical standards, being very frequently of the order of 4 to 5 percent for the gross national product (GNP). For instance, over the 1970-76 period the median GNP growth rate of the middle-income countries was 6.0 percent, or almost double that of the advanced economies for the same period, which was 3.2 percent. This is very high compared with growth rates of the nineteenth century. Even though population growth erodes the per capita gains made, it is important for spatial planning to determine where this increment of output will be located. The slowdown of the developing economies in the 1980s because of the energy crisis is unlikely to bring their economic growth rates to the nineteenth-century level.

In practically all developing countries the role of the state is dominant, so that a laissez-faire, do-nothing approach to the location of population and economic activities, similar to that of most advanced economies at comparable levels of urbanization, is in fact impossible. The government has an inevitable influence through its policies, the location of infrastructure investment, and the public enterprises that it controls. Because government is an important and sometimes even a dominant partner in the growth process, it must clarify its objectives and strategies. This does not mean that the state is relieved from all the economic constraints experienced by the private sector, but rather that a well-thought-out strategy is a requirement for more rapid progress. In many developing countries national spatial development is also marked by a higher degree of economic dualism and inequality among regions and urban areas. The rapid rate of growth of the urban population can lead to the concentration of large groups of low-income households in a few large cities. This in turn complicates the task of development. Effective settlement strategies may alleviate this problem.

In other words, the spatial distribution of population and economic activities has important implications for the efficiency of the economies as well as for the distribution of income and

---

2. As used in this book, the word "billion" means thousand million.

welfare and eventually for social stability in all countries. The urgent need for better strategies is accentuated in middle-income countries by the joint effect of their rapidly growing output and population. By the end of this century, if the output of a country grows at 5 percent a year, space will have to be provided for an economy 2.7 times greater in value than at present. If its population grows at 3 percent a year, space will have to be provided for 1.8 times more people than at present.

The Formulation of Appropriate Policy

The main determinants of urbanization and population concentration in urban areas are: the rate of development and the structure of the agricultural sector (which is heavily influenced by the size distribution of landholdings); the growth rate and sectoral pattern of industrialization; the location decisions affecting the distribution of manufacturing and therefore service activities among cities; and the condition of the transport and communication networks. Population redistribution and migration (hence, the patterns of urbanization) are the result of the creation of new employment opportunities.

Rapidly changing patterns of settlements create four major kinds of imbalances: between the rural and the urban sectors, between the level of development of different regions, between cities of different sizes, and between social groups within cities, particularly in large ones. Correspondingly, national urbanization policy has four major objectives: the full development of the national resources of the country; the maintenance of national cohesion among various regions, particularly in the case of very large disparities in per capita output among regions; the prevention or correction of excessive concentration of economic activities within the capital region; and the more efficient and more equitable management of growth within cities.

Appropriate national urbanization policies would eliminate the unintended and unwanted spatial effects of national economic policies and would promote the more efficient internal management of cities. They would also increase national economic efficiency and socioeconomic integration by eliminating interregional barriers to resource mobility, trade, and the diffusion of information and innovations.

Unintended spatial biases are commonly generated by national trade policies that protect the manufacturing sector; by credit allocations, public investment and subsidies, or pricing policies that give preferential treatment to economic activities concentrated in a few cities and regions; and by the management practices of the government and its regulation of economic activities. Of major significance is the place accorded to rural development and the farm sector in the national growth strategy. National urbanization policies must make sure that national economic and social policies do not accentuate sharply and unnecessarily the concentration of population and economic activities in large urban centers.

Appropriate management of all cities is very important to the success of a decentralization policy. In the case of very large cities, policies to limit or stop completely population growth are not a substitute for policies that directly address the problems of congestion and pollution and the inadequate provision of services for large segments of the population. If cities other than the capital are not efficiently and effectively managed, their chances of attracting industries and deflecting rural-urban as well as city-to-city migrants away from the capital region are very limited.

To limit population concentration in large urban centers, decentralization policies must encourage the growth of the farm sector as well as the growth of intermediate urban centers. Decentralization must be based on policies favorable to the farm sector because the stagnation of agriculture would slow the growth of provincial rural centers and small towns and would speed concentration in large cities. The more equal the distribution of income and assets in rural areas the greater will be the benefits of these policies. Decentralization policies must also encourage the development of intermediate-size urban centers with a good growth potential because economic goods and services, financial flows, and innovations circulate throughout the country via the system of cities. Secondary urban centers can be strengthened through appropriate transport policies, industrial estates policies, and, more important perhaps, the systematic development of organizational and informational networks between these cities and the capital region (such as banking networks, industrial and professional associations, and administrative structures). Such strategies are more a way of thinking about growth centers than a precise methodology. They move from a position of strength and concentrate on various forms of investment in the cities that already show promise for growth.

There are three major reasons for the frequent failure of national urbanization policies in developing countries. First and foremost is the lack of high-level political commitment to a better distribution of economic activities throughout the country. Second, urbanization policies fail because they concentrate exclusively on the problems of urban decentralization and ignore the fact that national economic policies (in such areas as trade, industry, and infrastructure) provide strong implicit incentives to locate in the dominant urban region. An additional shortcoming is that present urbanization policies seem to be a cheap way of avoiding the problems of internal inefficiency in the dominant urban region. The third typical cause of failure of settlements policies is the stop-and-go application of policy instruments according to short-term political or economic circumstances. Since location decisions by individual business firms are rather infrequent and represent a long-term commitment, stop-and-go policies are almost entirely discounted, and migrant workers will continue to go where the jobs are. National urbanization policies in some developing countries are only beginning to be stable enough and different enough that their experiences are worth comparing.

At low levels of urbanization and economic development, the concentration of population and economic activities in a few urban centers of small or medium size is inevitable if the national economy is to benefit from the positive effects of the concentration of resources, infrastructure, and services, which allows greater specialization and efficiency and in turn facilitates innovation. At that stage, the appropriate objective of a national urbanization strategy is to make sure that economic and social policies do not accentuate sharply and unnecessarily the concentration of political power and economic activities in these few cities. Socioeconomic policies can create strong biases in favor of the largest cities that cause a degree of concentration well above that which would otherwise take place, while growth of the hinterland is suppressed. Sound rural policies are most important at low levels of urbanization when the farm sector provides a large share of the national output. Excessive urban concentration because of past biases against the farm sector is difficult to correct until advanced stages of development.

In the middle-income countries with high population growth and dynamic economies, it is not realistic to expect that appropriate national urbanization policies will stop completely the growth of selected large cities in a short time (say, ten years). Many of these large cities already depend more on natural population growth than on migration for their expansion. An important threshold will already be crossed when net migration is reduced to zero. At present, the only countries experiencing net out-migration from the core regions are advanced economies characterized by very low national population growth rates (well under 1.5 percent), high levels of urbanization (well over 60 percent), and a high degree of business mobility because there are many locations with good potential in the country.

Outline of the Study

Chapter 2 presents a worldwide perspective on urbanization and shows how rates of urbanization in developing countries are consistently higher than the historical European and North American rates. It also shows the wide variations in the level of urbanization among the countries of the world and compares rates of change, the extent of urban concentration, and the number of very large cities in each. On the basis of this very aggregate information, it is possible to see common features in the evolution of patterns of settlements in groups of countries. The middle-income countries can benefit the most from active policies toward the distribution of population and economic activities because they are experiencing the most rapid changes and have the resources necessary to make a difference. The contrast between the various countries regrouped in a rather imperfect typology helps to clarify the priorities appropriate for national urbanization policy under various states of development.

The third chapter discusses the determinants of resource mobility within a country and the urbanization process. Much emphasis is placed on the process of reaching the decision to move in the case of business firms, individuals, and households. A better understanding of the decision to move is central to the formulation of sensible and effective policies aiming at rechanneling resources between regions and cities. Such an understanding of actual mobility patterns in developing countries will make possible the effective adaptation of the instruments and methods used in advanced economies. In the process, it also becomes clearer why economic development sets in motion a complex of forces that move both capital and labor toward favored locations and concentrate social and economic activities in cities, particularly large ones. Rural-urban interactions are examined to indicate why and how rural development policies are an integral part of properly conceived national urbanization strategies.

If the concentration of economic activities and large-scale urbanization are responses to the economic incentives generated by development, why is there a spatial development problem? Chapter 4 discusses the main forces pushing policymakers to develop national urbanization policies: the high concentration of population within the capital region, the need to maintain the cohesion of the country by preventing or reducing divergencies in the level of development and welfare of various regions, and the need to develop more fully the national resources located in peripheral regions. The relative importance of the spatial effects implicit in national economic policies is contrasted with that of the effects of policies explicitly addressed to the correction of spatial problems. The choice of appropriate policies to deal with excessive population concentration in large cities, lagging regions, or undeveloped areas is reviewed. The types of instruments available for carrying out policies are discussed with emphasis on their context: the structure of industry, national policies, the structure of government, and local government policies. Also stressed are the implicit spatial biases of national economic policies and the limitations they place on national urbanization policies.

The final chapter discusses the choice of appropriate policies under various circumstances. It defines some basic principles on the basis of past policy experiences. It also presents the policy measures that can be used at various levels of policymaking. Finally, it reviews the dominant issues in countries at various stages of urban development.

2

World Urbanization:
A Simple Typology for
National Urbanization Strategies

The facts about global trends in world population are becoming more and more widely known. The world population is estimated to have been approximately 800 million in 1750 and to have increased to about 1.3 billion by 1850; by 1950 it had grown to about 2.5 billion. Between 1950 and 1970 the world population grew by another 1.1 billion, to reach somewhat over 3.6 billion in 1970. Between 1970 and the end of the century it is expected that the world population will increase by about 80 percent, to reach a total of about 6.5 billion.[1] These striking figures are projections and, as such, are subject to error, but even though they may overestimate the world population for the year 2000, they imply extraordinary changes in the social and economic structure of most countries. The accompanying changes in the demographic structure are just as far-reaching as the projected total size of the world population: the majority of the world population is very young and potentially very mobile.[2]

The demographic changes of greatest interest to this discussion are those associated with the rapid pace of the rural-urban redistribution of the population and the equally important shifts in the proportion of the urban population living in very large cities. The definition of the urban population of a country is to some

---

1. Sidney Goldstein and David F. Sly, eds., *Patterns of Urbanization: Comparative Country Studies*, International Union for the Scientific Study of Population (IUSSP) Working Paper no. 3 (Dolhain, Brussels: Ordina Editions, 1977).
2. See the World Bank, *World Development Report, 1980* (New York: Oxford University Press, 1980), for indicators for the population under fifteen years of age.

degree arbitrary, and definitions change from country to country as well as over time within the same country. Some countries define as urban all human settlements of more than 2,500 people; others such as Japan or Korea for many purposes define cities as having populations of more than 50,000.[3] This creates problems of comparability between countries. Another caveat is that any population projection is merely an extrapolation of what would happen if certain assumptions concerning levels of mortality and fertility were realized. The element of uncertainty is increased in the case of rural-urban projections because rural-urban migration is susceptible to rapid and sometimes erratic changes, which can always be explained after the fact but not necessarily anticipated. The projections discussed below must be considered as indicators of things to come. The patterns are unmistakable even if the risk of error is substantial in the case of a single city.

Worldwide Trends

Demographic research has shown that before 1850 no country was predominantly urban. As late as 1900 only Great Britain had crossed that threshold. By 1920 about 14 percent of the world population was urbanized, but by the year 2000 it is expected that more than 50 percent of the world population will be urbanized. The world trend toward urbanization is approximately as follows:

Year	Percent urban	Year	Percent urban
1920	14.3	1960	33.0
1930	16.3	1970	37.2
1940	18.3	1980	41.5
1950	25.4	1990	46.1
		2000	51.1

In the more detailed description that follows, both the past record and the current U.N. projections to the year 2000 are presented. It must be reemphasized that the projections reported are speculative. To restate an earlier warning:

Changes in current and projected patterns of national increase

---

3. For more details on definitions of urban population, refer to United Nations, Manual VIII, *Methods for Projections of Urban and Rural Populations*, U.N. Population Studies no. 55 (New York, 1977).

Table 1. *Average Annual Rates of Increase in Rural, Urban, and Total World Population*

Year	Total population			Urban population			Rural population		
	World total	More developed regions	Less developed regions	World total	More developed regions	Less developed regions	World total	More developed regions	Less developed regions
1955	1.75	1.30	1.99	3.40	2.49	4.88	1.07	−0.06	1.40
1960	1.89	1.28	2.18	3.47	2.40	5.01	1.14	−0.18	1.50
1965	1.96	1.22	2.31	3.02	2.18	4.09	1.42	−0.20	1.81
1970	1.92	0.88	2.39	2.93	1.96	4.07	1.36	−0.93	1.86
1975	1.93	0.88	2.36	3.05	1.76	4.38	1.25	−0.84	1.65
1980	1.97	0.87	2.39	3.05	1.69	4.29	1.25	−0.94	1.62
1985	1.98	0.85	2.37	3.02	1.61	4.15	1.22	−1.05	1.55
1990	1.91	0.76	2.29	2.91	1.45	3.95	1.12	−1.21	1.42
1995	1.86	0.67	2.22	2.81	1.29	3.76	1.02	−1.36	1.30
2000	1.76	0.62	2.08	2.69	1.18	3.53	0.88	−1.47	1.11

Source: United Nations, Population Division, *Urban-Rural Projections from 1950 to 2000,* Working Paper no. 10 (New York, October 9, 1974).

and migration, errors in existing data, and in some places the lack of data, as well as changes in urban definitions all contribute a degree of uncertainty to the precision of existing data. While each of these sources of error can contribute independently to the total in the estimates, their effects on projections can be even more serious as the initial impacts become compounded through time in the projection process.[4]

The relative growth rates of rural and urban population are presented in table 1. This table shows the average annual rate of change in the world urban and rural population as well as the comparable average rates of change of more and less developed countries separately. The urban growth rates of developing countries have been and are projected to continue to be twice as high as the urban growth rate of more developed countries. They are projected to be three times as high by the last decade of the century.

By the end of the century the world urban population is expected to be greater than 3.3 billion. If this projection is anywhere near correct it implies that, while the total world population will have increased by about 80 percent over the 1970-2000 period, the urban population will have increased by about 145 percent.[5] In the entire second half of the century (1950-2000) the world population is expected to grow by about 160 percent and the urban population by an enormous 375 percent. The world population will require about thirty-five years to double once, while the urban population will take about forty-five years to double twice. By contrast, the rural population is not expected even to double during the same fifty-year period; it is expected to increase by about 80 percent.

Whatever the degree of error carried by the current projections and the various possible definitions of urbanization, the world-wide implications of the figures are:

— Urban areas will play an increasing role in absorbing large shares of the world population.

4. Goldstein and Sly, *Patterns of Urbanization*, p. 47.
5. The main cause for caution is that the People's Republic of China represents about one-fourth of the world population, and at the time of this writing accurate and reliable demographic information was not yet available from that country.

— There will be a marked increase in the level of urbanization. An increasingly large number of countries will have
become more urban than rural.
— Even though the world population will not become more
urban than rural until the end of the century, by 1978
there were already more countries predominantly urban
rather than rural.
— The distribution of urban population among regions of the
world has changed drastically for cities of more than 100,000.
At the beginning of the century the largest share of the
world urban population was found in Europe. Since 1950
Europe has had only the third largest share, after Asia and
the Americas. Asia will dominate the world picture with about
45 percent of the world urban population by the year 2000.

Sources of Urban Growth

The statistics on urban population can change because of the
natural growth of the population already living in cities, the net
rate of in-migration, or the redrawing of city boundaries with the
annexation of nearby towns. At present, the components of urban
change have been calculated only on the basis of 1960 data by
the United Nations because of serious problems in doing accurate growth accounting for a widely different set of countries.
The comparison of the aggregate results shows that natural increase has been playing a greater role in the growth of urban areas
in developing countries than in advanced economies, in spite of
the fact that net migration was also higher in the developing
countries. This was because in 1960 the birthrates observed in
urban areas in developing countries were only 15 percent below
those of rural areas; in both cases, these rates were several orders
of magnitude higher than in advanced economies. More recent
demographic analysis suggests that population growth rates are
declining in developing countries. Efforts to control fertility will
have a direct positive effect on the rate of urban growth and on
the potential for population deconcentration.

The net transfer of population from rural to urban places in
less developed areas is still low, however; only 5.9 persons in 1,000
of the rural population moved to urban places in 1960. At present,
"the very large and still rapidly growing rural population provides

a tremendous reservoir of potential migrants to cities."[6] The extraordinary growth of urban areas should not distract from the fact that many countries have large rural populations, even though a large proportion (about 40 percent) of their urban population still live in towns of less than 100,000. Rapidly growing large cities coexist with a large population living in rural villages and small towns. Because very large cities dominate the urban system, there is a great difference between the average size and the typical size of settlements. Despite large urban agglomerations, most settlements are typically rural, with important implications for rural development.

With respect to the population of large cities (defined as cities of more than a million inhabitants) the prospects for developed and developing countries are quite different. In developed countries the size of the urban population is expected to be about 2.7 times larger in 1985 than it was in 1950. In developing countries the urban population in cities of more than a million will increase ten times during the same period.

Level of Urbanization

The level of urbanization of a country, that is, the percentage of population living in urban areas, is the first major indicator to consider in cross-country comparisons of national urbanization policies. There are several reasons for paying attention to the level of urbanization. First, at low levels of urbanization, economic and settlements policies should be dominated by a concern for the rural sector. Second, there is a close association between the level of urbanization and the level of economic development as measured by the per capita GNP (see figure 1). Third, at low levels of urbanization, rural-urban migration is the main source of growth of the urban sector; at high levels, the main source of total urban growth is the natural increase of the resident population. There are significant differences among countries, but it is not entirely misleading to examine regional breakdowns because geographic contiguity is often associated with comparable levels of urbanization. The countries are regrouped here according to the regions used by the United Nations. Heterogeneous levels of urbanization

6. Goldstein and Sly, *Patterns of Urbanization*, p. 64.

Figure 1. Level of Urbanization and per Capita GNP

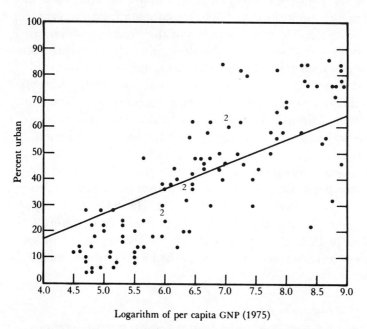

Logarithm of per capita GNP (1975)

Note: The number 2 refers to two identical observations. The sample contained 111 countries but only 106 are plotted; five outlyers are not on the chart. Estimated equation: Percent urban $-20.845 + 9.558$ in GNP per capita. $R^2 = 0.456$.

Source: William Dillinger, "A National Urban Data File for 114 Countries," Urban and Regional Report no. 79-5 (Washington, D.C.: Urban and Regional Economics Division, World Bank, 1979).

are indicated when they occur within a given region. For convenience, the complete listing of the countries found in each region and subregion is presented in figure 2; names and countries correspond to the year 1975.

Africa. Africa is the least urbanized region of the world, and the cities there have the smallest urban population in the world. By the year 2000 the entire region will still remain the least urbanized of the world (about 40 percent). There are such great differences among the subregions, however, that this regional average is misleading. The northern and southern regions (12 and 13) were already close to or past the 50 percent mark in 1978, when the other regions were not past the 25 percent mark and will barely pass that level by the year 2000. A note of caution should be sounded for the Middle Africa region (11), which is projected to cross the 50 percent level by the year 2000: the demographic base of this area is one of the weakest anywhere. Between sub-regions there are sharp differences in the contribution of natural increase to the total growth in urban population. The contribution of natural population increase is the highest in the northern region, which contains most of the very large cities of the continent, and this region should be separated in a finer breakdown.

Latin America. During the past twenty-five years only the Soviet Union has been urbanizing at a faster pace than Latin America. Urban growth rates in Latin America have been about four times higher than rural growth rates. By the year 2000 the continent as a whole will be more than 75 percent urbanized, will have reached the level of North America in 1975, and will be at a level of urbanization comparable with that of Europe. Urbanization is expected to advance at very different paces in the four subregions. Tropical South America will change very rapidly and reach the levels of temperate South America, leaving the other two regions behind. As discussed below, population concentration in the largest cities is a particularly significant feature of Latin American urbanization.

Asia. The Asian region is probably the most heterogeneous of all regions. Because of the dominance of India, Indonesia, and China, it combines a very low level of urbanization with the largest absolute urban population in the world—already double the size of that of North America, itself the most urbanized region of the world. During the past twenty-five years East Asia has begun differentiating itself from the rest of the region because of the combined effect of rapid economic growth and falling population growth rates. In South Asia, India's unique type of urbanization combines a very low and stable level of urbanization over long periods with a numerically large urban sector. Projections suggest that the pace of urbanization in India might accelerate during the last quarter of this century. For purposes of policy analysis, the countries of the South Asia region fall into markedly different groups. (In particular, the Western South Asia group as defined by the United Nations has more in common with Northern Africa than with the rest of South Asia.)

Figure 2. Country Groupings Used for Demographic Analysis
by the U.N. Population Division, 1975

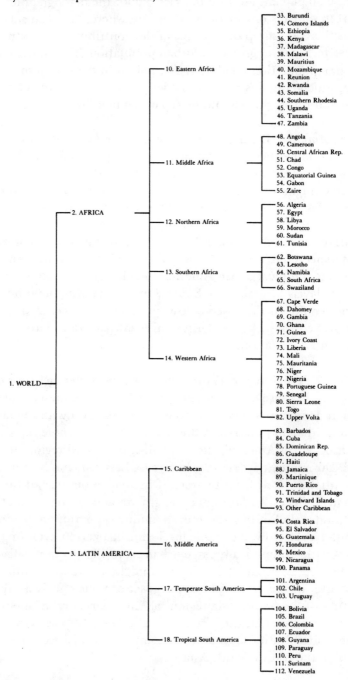

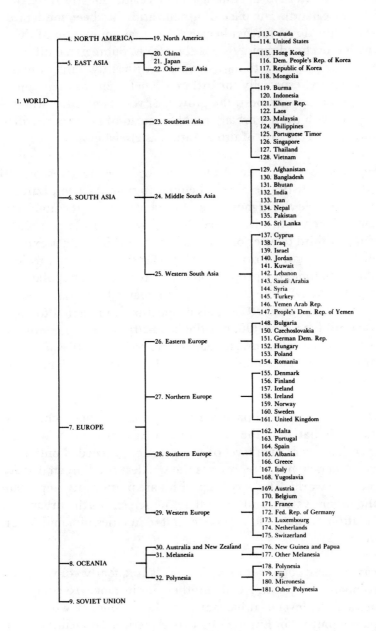

- 1. WORLD
  - 4. NORTH AMERICA — 19. North America
    - 113. Canada
    - 114. United States
  - 5. EAST ASIA
    - 20. China
    - 21. Japan
    - 22. Other East Asia
      - 115. Hong Kong
      - 116. Dem. People's Rep. of Korea
      - 117. Republic of Korea
      - 118. Mongolia
  - 6. SOUTH ASIA
    - 23. Southeast Asia
      - 119. Burma
      - 120. Indonesia
      - 121. Khmer Rep.
      - 122. Laos
      - 123. Malaysia
      - 124. Philippines
      - 125. Portuguese Timor
      - 126. Singapore
      - 127. Thailand
      - 128. Vietnam
    - 24. Middle South Asia
      - 129. Afghanistan
      - 130. Bangladesh
      - 131. Bhutan
      - 132. India
      - 133. Iran
      - 134. Nepal
      - 135. Pakistan
      - 136. Sri Lanka
    - 25. Western South Asia
      - 137. Cyprus
      - 138. Iraq
      - 139. Israel
      - 140. Jordan
      - 141. Kuwait
      - 142. Lebanon
      - 143. Saudi Arabia
      - 144. Syria
      - 145. Turkey
      - 146. Yemen Arab Rep.
      - 147. People's Dem. Rep. of Yemen
  - 7. EUROPE
    - 26. Eastern Europe
      - 148. Bulgaria
      - 150. Czechoslovakia
      - 151. German Dem. Rep.
      - 152. Hungary
      - 153. Poland
      - 154. Romania
    - 27. Northern Europe
      - 155. Denmark
      - 156. Finland
      - 157. Iceland
      - 158. Ireland
      - 159. Norway
      - 160. Sweden
      - 161. United Kingdom
    - 28. Southern Europe
      - 162. Malta
      - 163. Portugal
      - 164. Spain
      - 165. Albania
      - 166. Greece
      - 167. Italy
      - 168. Yugoslavia
    - 29. Western Europe
      - 169. Austria
      - 170. Belgium
      - 171. France
      - 172. Fed. Rep. of Germany
      - 173. Luxembourg
      - 174. Netherlands
      - 175. Switzerland
  - 8. OCEANIA
    - 30. Australia and New Zealand
    - 31. Melanesia
      - 176. New Guinea and Papua
      - 177. Other Melanesia
    - 32. Polynesia
      - 178. Polynesia
      - 179. Fiji
      - 180. Micronesia
      - 181. Other Polynesia
  - 9. SOVIET UNION

Europe. Europe has the third highest level of urbanization
in the world after North America and Oceania (mostly Australia
and New Zealand). The pace of urbanization has been moderate
and will slow down further because the rural population of the
region has declined rapidly since the 1950s. Subregional differences are projected to narrow very significantly during the rest
of the century, especially the difference between Northern and
Southern Europe. At best, the growth of very large cities will
keep pace with overall urban growth, instead of being more than
double the overall rate of urbanization as elsewhere.

Soviet Union. The case of the Soviet Union is treated separately
in the U.N. statistics because it belongs to both Asia and Europe.
It has combined the highest rate of urbanization of the nine U.N.
regions of the world with a very slow growth of the largest cities.
During the third quarter of the century, the U.S.S.R. has experienced a higher rate of rural-urban transfer than any other region.
At the same time, the proportion of the total urban population
found in cities of more than a million remained very small—less
than 15 percent until 1970. This proportion is projected to increase until the year 2000, but the large-city share will continue
to remain small by world standards. The relation between a
centrally planned economic system and this type of urbanization
is discussed later.

Oceania. The overall pattern of growth in Oceania is completely dominated by the experience of Australia and New Zealand. It has a very high level of urbanization, exceeded only by
North America, but it represents the smallest total urban population of the world. The very large cities are particularly important
to the urban system, and more than 50 percent of the urban
population of this region is concentrated in cities of a million or
more.

Thirty-three countries or regions. It is frequently convenient
to compare one country with another; for instance, to compare
changes in the level of urbanization in Latin America with the
historical pattern in Europe or North America. To facilitate such
comparisons, thirty-three graphs of individual countries or groups
of countries are given in figure 3. They indicate that the rates of

Figure 3. Level of Urbanization in Thirty-three Countries and Regions

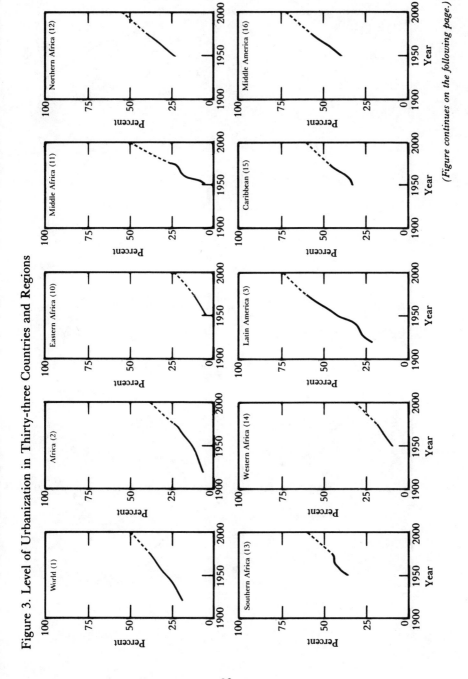

(*Figure continues on the following page.*)

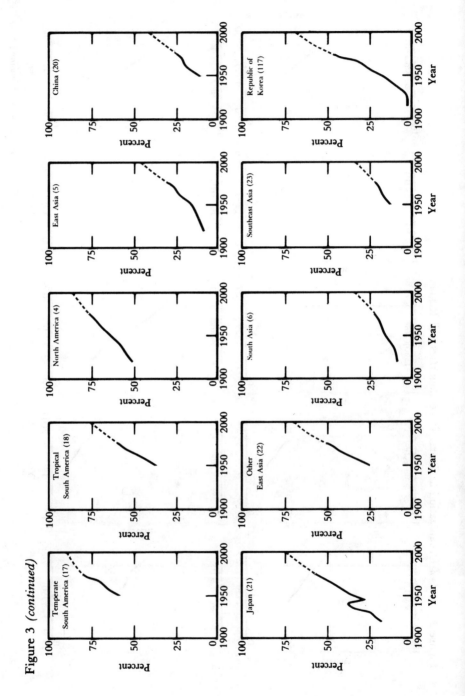

Figure 3 (continued)

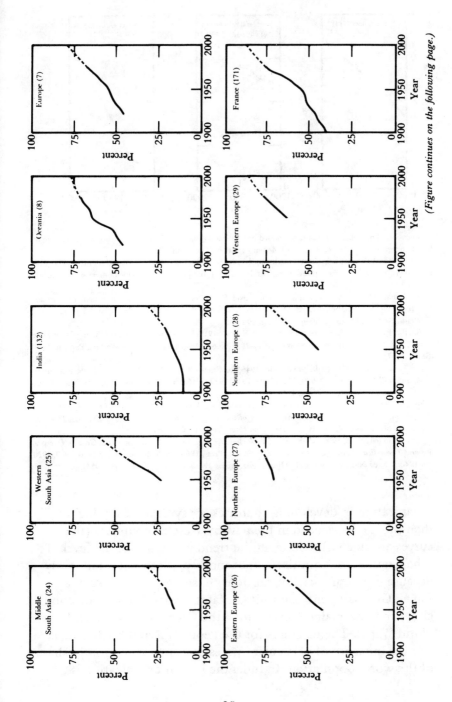

(Figure continues on the following page.)

25

Figure 3 *(continued)*

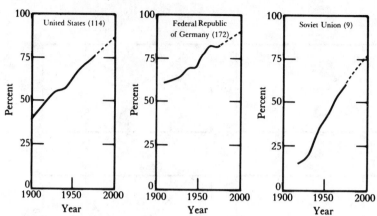

Note: Solid line indicates actuals, and dotted line indicates projections. Numbers in parentheses refer to the listing in figure 2. For the countries included in each region, see figure 2.

Source: For 1950 through 2000, for all regions and individual countries: United Nations, *Urban-Rural Projections from 1950 to 2000* (New York, October 9, 1974; computer printout), medium term with medium variant.

For India, 1901-71: Sidney Goldstein and David F. Sly, eds., *Patterns of Urbanization: Comparative Country Studies,* International Union for the Scientific Study of Population (IUSSP) Working Paper no. 3 (Dolhain, Belgium: Ordina Editions, 1977), p. 295.

For the Republic of Korea (including North Korea), 1915-45: Edwin S. Mills and Byung Nack Song, *Korea's Urbanization and Urban Problems, 1945-1975,* Korea Development Institute Working Paper no. 7701 (Seoul, 1977).

For Japan, 1920, 1925, 1930, 1935, 1940, 1945; for France, 1901, 1906, 1911, 1921, 1926, 1931, 1936, 1946; and for West Germany, 1900, 1910, 1925, 1933, 1939, 1946: United Nations, Statistical Office, *Demographic Yearbook, 1952* (New York, 1954).

For Europe, North America, Soviet Union, Oceania, East Asia, South Asia, Latin America, and Africa, 1920, 1930, and 1940: United Nations, *Growth of the World's Urban and Rural Population, 1920-2000,* Population Studies no. 44, ST/SOA/Series A/44 (New York, 1970), p. 49.

For the United States, 1900: Allan Pred, *The Spatial Dynamics of U.S. Urban-Industrial Growth: Interpretive and Theoretical Essays* (Cambridge, Mass.: M.I.T. Press, 1966), table 2-1, p. 17; for 1910, 1920, 1930, and 1940: United Nations, Statistical Office, *Demographic Yearbook, 1952* (New York, 1954).

urbanization in developing countries are systematically higher than those experienced in the past by Western countries (the curves are steeper). Although the trend is very clear, the level of urbanization does not rise monotonously; it can fall temporarily because of major social disruptions. In some countries such as Japan, Germany, and the United States the level of urbanization either fell or remained level during the Great Depression and World War II. The diagrams for the People's Republic of China and for India are of particular interest because of their large share of the world population. In India the rate of urbanization is accelerating after a long flat trend; in China the rate of urbanization is significantly faster than in India and comparable to the long-term U.S. trend.

Tempo of Urbanization

The speed at which a country is urbanizing reflects the pressures on the urban sector and conditions in the policy environment. The United Nations calculates the tempo of urbanization for each country as the difference between the rate of growth of the urban population and that of the rural population. Under the practical but oversimplifying assumption that this tempo is stable, it is possible to project the level of urbanization. In any case, the observed difference between the rate of urban and that of rural population growth is a good indicator of the speed at which urbanization is taking place.[7] Over the 1950-70 period, for which actual data are available, the value of the urban-rural growth differential ranges from -0.41 for the United Kingdom to 10.35 for Papua New Guinea. In table 2 the data are presented for the countries with a population of more than 15 million in 1950. Among the fastest urbanizing countries were Ethiopia, Brazil, Korea, and Turkey. The figure for China is conjectural. (The complete results are presented in Appendix D, table D-1 for 1950-70, and table D-3 for 1970-75.)

There are four ways a country can have a very high value for the urban-rural growth differential: (1) a country at a low level of urbanization can have a high rate of urban growth because the absolute base is very small (the case of Papua New Guinea); (2) a country may have a high rate of urban growth because of international migration combined with a declining rural population (the case of Singapore and Hong Kong); (3) a country can have a high rate of urbanization combined with a rapidly declining rural population and a total population growth rate which is falling (the case of Korea); and (4) a country may have a high total population growth rate and a high rate of farm out-migration with its rural population still growing (the case of Algeria). Among developing countries, the first and fourth type of high urbanization rates are

7. A better indicator might be the percentage of urban population growth attributable to rural-urban migration, but even for a single country it is more difficult to compute precisely.

Table 2. *Tempo of Urbanization between 1950 and 1970 for
all Countries with a Population Greater than 15 Million in 1950*

Country	Total population (millions)		Urban-rural growth differential, 1950-70
	1950	1970	
Africa			
Egypt	20.5	33.3	2.66
Ethiopia	17.7	24.8	5.50
Nigeria	34.3	46.1	2.60
South America			
Argentina	17.1	23.7	3.18
Brazil	52.0	95.2	3.89
Mexico	26.3	50.5	3.37
North America			
United States	152.3	204.9	2.37
Asia			
Bangladesh	40.0	68.2	1.79
Burma	18.3	27.7	3.03
China	540.3	771.8	3.79
India	359.2	548.4	1.11
Indonesia	76.0	120.0	2.32
Iran	16.6	28.4	2.59
Japan	82.9	104.3	3.61
Korea (North and South)	30.1	44.6	5.27
Korea, Dem. Rep. of	9.7	13.9	4.33
Korea, Rep. of	20.3	30.7	5.71
Pakistan	36.6	62.0	2.68
Philippines	20.3	38.4	1.38
Thailand	19.6	36.2	1.99
Turkey	20.8	35.6	4.11
Vietnam	24.6	33.2	2.65
Europe			
Germany, Fed. Rep. of	47.8	60.7	2.13
France	41.7	50.7	3.72
German Dem. Rep.	18.4	17.0	.07
Italy	46.8	53.6	2.04
Poland	24.8	32.5	3.01
Romania	16.3	20.2	3.47
Spain	27.9	33.8	2.89
United Kingdom	50.6	55.5	−0.41
Yugoslavia	16.3	20.4	3.27
Soviet Union	180.0	242.0	3.48

Source: United Nations, *Urban-Rural Projections from 1950 to 2000* (New York,
October 9, 1974; computer printout), medium term with medium variant.

the most common. The first type is characteristic of many African countries with low levels of urbanization. The fourth type shows the potent effect of rapid population growth when combined with rapid economic growth.

An important aspect of urbanization in developing countries is that few countries so far have been experiencing an absolute decline in the rural population. The decline of the farm population is a clear sign that the economy has become predominantly urban in character and that the urban labor markets have become the main determinant of employment. The source of growth of specific cities is less and less rural-to-urban migration, but rather the movement of population from city to city. This indicator alone signals the need for a specific national settlements policy focusing on interurban mobility. The developing countries in such a situation are still few: Singapore, Hong Kong, Venezuela, Republic of Korea, Bulgaria, Chile, Uruguay, Jamaica, Argentina, and Greece.

The role of international migration in the rate of urbanization has been generally limited worldwide. It has operated in two ways. First, some countries have experienced higher rates of urbanization because of international migration; they are small and among the fastest urbanizing countries: Singapore, Kuwait, Hong Kong, Venezuela, Ivory Coast, and Saudi Arabia. Second, a few countries have benefited from international migration that has slowed the growth of their rural population, as in Portugal, which sent migrants to countries of the European Economic Community (compensated in part by returnees from Angola). In some advanced countries substantial rates of urbanization were observed because of the very rapid rate of decline of the rural population in 1950-70; this is particularly clear in the case of France, Japan, and Sweden.

Components of Urban Growth

The relative importance of the two major components of urban growth—natural increase of the urban population and rural-urban migration—is of major significance to policymakers. In preparing policies designed to affect the mobility of labor and firms throughout the urban system, it makes a great deal of difference whether the major source of urban growth is net in-migration or natural

Table 3. *Share of Net Migration in Urban Growth, 1970-75*

Country	Urban growth	Share of migration	Population growth
Papua New Guinea	10.1	74.3	2.6
Yemen Arab Republic	8.0	76.3	1.9
Kuwait	8.2	24.4	6.2
Tanzania	7.5	64.0	2.7
Nigeria	7.0	64.3	2.5
Colombia	4.9	43.1	2.8
Mexico	4.6	23.4	3.5
Brazil	4.5	35.5	2.9
Venezuela	3.9	20.5	3.1
Argentina	2.0	35.0	1.3
Thailand	5.3	45.3	2.9
Philippines	4.8	41.7	2.8
Indonesia	4.7	48.9	2.4
Sri Lanka	4.3	60.5	2.1
India	3.8	44.7	1.7
Bulgaria	2.8	82.1	0.5
U.S.S.R.	2.4	62.1	0.9
Poland	2.2	59.1	0.9
Hungary	1.5	73.3	0.5
German Dem. Rep.	0.5	160.0	-0.3
France	1.8	55.5	0.8
Sweden	1.2	66.7	0.4
Belgium	1.0	70.0	0.3
Germany, Fed. Rep. of	0.8	75.0	0.2
United Kingdom	0.5	60.0	0.2

Source: United Nations, *Urban-Rural Projections from 1950 to 2000.*

urban growth. Unfortunately, to be accurate, an analysis of the components of urban growth requires the use of separate information on fertility and mortality in cities, on the age structure of the population, and on urban annexation through the redrawing of city boundaries. The last comprehensive analytical effort was carried out for 1960 by the United Nations, and a new analysis is currently in progress for 1970. The distinction between rural-urban migration and natural urban growth is important because rural-urban migration and urban-to-urban (city-to-city) migration decisions are made quite differently.

    In the absence of a more precise demographic analysis, orders of magnitude for the percentage of urban growth from net rural-urban migration have been estimated for 1970-75. This percentage has been obtained by taking the difference between the urban growth rate and the national growth rate and dividing it by the urban growth rate.[8] The results show that the contribution of rural-urban migration to urban growth is generally significant (see table 3). It is particularly high at low levels of urbanization and at very high levels of urbanization, but for very different reasons. In advanced economies rural-urban migration is proportionately large because both urban and total population growth are very low. This is particularly conspicuous in the case of the German Democratic Republic, where the proportion is 160 percent, because cities continue to grow very slowly when the national population has been declining. The situation is rather similar for advanced centrally planned economies. In Latin American countries, the natural increase of the urban population is the dominant force behind urban growth. This is also the case in Southeast Asia and South Asia, but for different reasons: in these regions the nonfarm sectors are not dynamic enough to stimulate rapid migration, and they are still at a low level of urbanization. Kuwait is exceptional because it is growing through international immigration. To complete the sample of twenty-five countries presented in table 3, the full results are presented for 125 areas in Appendix D, table D-2. In that table the share of migration to that of urban growth ranges from 160 percent for the German Democratic Republic to - 11.7 percent for Hong Kong.

Extent of Population Concentration in Large Cities

The concern for the problems of urbanization is directed increasingly at the concentration of population in cities of more than a million or in even larger cities of 2 million or more. This trend is evident in the demographic analyses produced by the United Nations. The aggregate data in table 4 make it clear that larger and larger cities are increasing their share of the total urban population; more detailed information is given in table 5. Very tentatively, the United Nations projects the number of cities of more than 5 million to increase from twenty-one to fifty-nine, with two-thirds of them in developing countries. These numbers

---

8. It is only a first approximation to the contribution of net migration to urbanization because it assumes (1) that there are no fertility nor mortality differentials between the rural and the urban sectors, (2) that the redrawing of city boundaries and annexation of rural areas is insignificant, and (3) that the minimum threshold size for reclassification of areas from rural to urban has no effect on the results.

Table 4. *Percentage Share of Total Urban Population by Each Size Class of Large Cities*

City size (thousands)	Percentage share by year		
	1950	1975	2000
5,000 or more	12.1 ⎱	19.9 ⎱	29.8 ⎱
2,000-4,999	18.6 ⎬ 45.1[a]	16.4 ⎬ 51.4[a]	18.6 ⎬ 62.7[a]
1,000-1,999	14.4 ⎰	15.1 ⎰	14.3 ⎰
500-999	17.6	15.6	12.6
200-499	21.7	20.2	15.3
100-199	15.6	12.8	9.4
Total	100.0	100.0	100.0
Total urban population	393 million	983 million	2,167 million

a. All cities of more than 1 million.
Source: Table 5.

are tentative in part because two or several adjacent cities can effectively form one continuous urbanized region of great magnitude.[9]

Large Cities and Primacy

Within a given country the concentration of the urban population in a few cities (primacy) and the existence of very large cities (of, say, 2 million to 3 million people) are not entirely distinguishable. But a country can experience primacy without having any very large city, while another country can have very large cities without exhibiting such primacy. Although problems of primacy cannot be overlooked in the formulation of national urbanization policies, the problems associated with very large cities are generally more important. The national context will determine the appropriate degree of emphasis.

The extent of primacy for 113 countries in 1975 is presented in table 6. The measure used is the ratio of the population of the largest city to the total urban population of the country. It is easy to compute and is not restricted by sample sizes or minimum city-size cutoff points. Except for the two city-states of Hong Kong and Singapore, most of the countries with a high primacy value are in the early stage of development.

9. For a discussion of this coalescence of urban areas, see Jean Gottmann, "Megapolitan Systems around the World," *Ekistics*, vol 243 (February 1976).

Table 5. *Size Distribution of Cities in Developed and Developing Countries, 1950-2000*

City size (thousands)	1950	1960	1970	1975	1980	1990	2000
			Number of cities				
World total							
5,000 or more	6	12	20	21	26	40	59
2,000-4,999	24	31	39	55	71	101	133
1,000-1,999	41	67	98	105	128	181	222
500-999	101	136	179	220	249	303	396
200-499	281	385	554	659	730	877	1,059
100-199	453	654	841	907	998	1,192	1,460
More developed regions							
5,000 or more	5	10	11	11	11	15	16
2,000-4,999	15	16	20	24	31	41	50
1,000-1,999	28	38	54	56	67	77	84
500-999	61	82	99	110	118	131	152
200-499	173	221	288	327	353	387	404
100-199	275	350	437	453	483	532	563
Less developed regions							
5,000 or more	1	2	9	10	15	25	43
2,000-4,999	9	15	19	31	40	60	83
1,000-1,999	13	29	44	49	61	104	138
500-999	40	54	80	110	131	172	244
200-499	108	164	266	332	377	490	655
100-199	178	304	404	454	515	660	897

(Table continues on following pages)

Table 5 (*continued*)

City size (thousands)	1950	1960	1970	1975	1980	1990	2000
			Population in cities (thousands)				
World total							
5,000 or more	47,364	95,951	167,219	195,761	251,519	414,403	646,485
2,000-4,999	73,026	92,219	114,011	161,706	206,072	297,200	403,079
1,000-1,999	56,314	94,591	137,429	148,378	173,533	243,965	309,962
500-999	69,062	95,949	124,336	153,846	171,701	208,403	273,641
200-499	84,568	117,838	168,667	198,040	222,250	274,458	330,575
100-199	61,713	90,845	118,858	125,503	138,130	167,311	203,788
More developed regions							
5,000 or more	41,583	83,019	103,145	112,169	121,354	159,486	182,552
2,000-4,999	48,306	43,744	57,659	70,485	90,619	115,869	147,637
1,000-1,999	39,434	54,272	75,016	79,590	91,504	103,835	114,603
500-999	41,630	56,839	68,715	78,752	81,083	89,456	103,784
200-499	53,286	68,339	86,965	99,018	106,354	120,803	128,268
100-199	37,535	48,950	61,698	63,147	66,168	73,294	79,487
Less developed regions							
5,000 or more	5,781	12,932	64,074	83,592	130,165	254,917	463,933
2,000-4,999	24,720	48,475	56,352	91,221	115,453	181,331	255,442
1,000-1,999	16,880	40,319	62,413	68,788	82,029	140,130	195,359
500-999	27,432	39,110	55,621	75,094	90,618	118,947	169,857
200-499	31,282	49,499	81,702	99,022	115,896	153,655	202,307
100-199	24,178	41,895	57,160	62,356	71,962	94,017	124,301

Source: United Nations, Population Division, Department of Economic and Social Affairs, *Trends and Prospects in the Population of Urban Agglomeration, 1950-2000*, ESA/P/WP50 (New York, November 1975).

Table 6. Degree of Urban Concentration Ranked by the Primacy Index

Place	Index	Place	Index	Place	Index	Place	Index
Hong Kong	100	Argentina	45	Sudan	33	Indonesia	21
Singapore	100	Korea, Rep. of	45	Afghanistan	32	Japan	21
Mozambique	88	Peru	45	Syria	32	Sri Lanka	21
Burundi	75	Rhodesia	45	Bangladesh	31	Sweden	20
Lebanon	72	Uganda	44	Finland	31	Switzerland	20
Jamaica	66	Nicaragua	43	Papua New Guinea	31	Taiwan	19
Senegal	65	Benin	42	Zaire	30	Germany, Fed. Rep. of	19
Uruguay	62	Jordan	42	Ghana	30	Turkey	19
Laos	61	Dominican Republic	41	Iran	30	Nigeria	18
Ivory Coast	60	El Salvador	40	Mexico	30	Romania	18
Malawi	60	Guinea	40	Niger	30	Canada	17
Paraguay	59	Israel	40	Yemen Arab Republic	30	Korea, Dem. Rep. of	17
Togo	58	Chad[a]	39	Zambia	29	Belgium	16
Haiti	56	Cuba	39	Morocco	28	Italy	16
Angola	55	Egypt	39	New Zealand	28	Malaysia	16
Libya	55	Guatemala	39	Philippines	28	Poland	16
Chile	54	Hungary	39	Vietnam	28	Brazil	15
Greece	54	Saudi Arabia	38	Venezuela	27	Spain	15
Costa Rica	53	Honduras	36	Albania	26	Algeria	14
Ireland	51	Norway	36	Australia	25	South Africa	13
Portugal	51	Burma	35	Pakistan	24	Czechoslovakia	11
Somalia	51	Denmark	35	United Kingdom	24	Yugoslavia	11
Tanzania	51	Tunisia	35	Upper Volta	24	Netherlands	10
Iraq	50	Bolivia	34	France	23	United States	10
Sierra Leone	50	Ecuador	34	Mali	23	German Dem. Rep.	9
Kenya	48	Madagascar[a]	34	Bulgaria	21	China	6
Austria	47	Kampuchea[a]	33	Cameroon	21	India	6
Rwanda	47	Ethiopia	33	Colombia	21	U.S.S.R.	5
Thailand	47	Nepal	33				

Note: The primacy index is the ratio of the population of the largest city to the total urban population.
a. Data not reliable.
Source: Based on United Nations, Demographic Yearbook, 1976, and indigenous sources.

There are other ways to estimate the level of primacy and to investigate the size distribution of cities in a country. The most traditional primacy measure consists in taking the ratio of the largest city in the country to the next three largest cities. This index is of particular value in showing the presence or absence of alternative urban centers large enough to balance the influence of the largest city. Estimates based on the U.N. *Demographic Yearbook* of 1976 are presented in Appendix D, table D-4. A more systematic method consists of fitting curves to the size distribution of cities to investigate the degree of development of the urban system.[10]

Factors Affecting National Spatial Development

The level of urbanization and its rate of change, rural-urban migration and the contribution of migration to urban growth, the differentiated growth of cities according to size, and the size distribution of cities are all important for the formulation of national settlements policy. They constitute major indicators of what is happening, but they *reveal* rather than *explain* the changing patterns of population distribution. It is useful to review the various factors which affect the spatial development of a country before separating the 182 countries and areas listed in figure 2 into groups relevant for the discussion of national urbanization policy. In evaluating the ability of a country to carry out specific policies, physical and demographic constraints are important. In addition, the economic resources available and the national economic priorities determine the range of national urbanization policies that can be useful. And ultimately, the political and institutional context determines how these policies will be carried out.

Physical Constraints

The total area of a country is an important dimension of national urbanization policy: large countries require higher infrastructure expenditure per capita to achieve spatial, political, and economic integration. The net population density based on

10. See Harvey Rosen and Steven Resnick, "The Size-Distribution of Cities: The Pareto Law and Primate Size" (Princeton University, February 1978; processed).

arable land is associated with a somewhat higher degree of urban concentration. The distribution of water resources also constrains urbanization and patterns of urban settlements. Island states (such as Caribbean states, the Philippines, Indonesia, and Pacific islands) confront special problems of population distribution and spatial integration. At the lower end of the geographical scale, very small countries are like city-states in that international migration can become important. In addition, the total population growth and urban- and rural-specific growth rates are major determinants of the growth rate of cities and the problems they encounter.

Economic Capacity

The level of GNP per capita is an essential factor for the formulation of policies: countries (such as those rich in minerals) enjoying a relatively high GNP per capita for their level of urbanization are in a particularly good position to undertake national urbanization policies. The rate of growth of the economy (especially gross investment) is another important factor because, without growth, few economic activities can be decentralized.[11] A skewed distribution of income and assets in rural and urban areas will contribute to the premature mobility of low-income households and will be a major brake on decentralization. Inequality will also be reflected in the size of the gap between the regional incomes of rich and poor regions.

The structure of trade is also a significant factor. Exploring the relation between the structure of the economy and the level of urbanization with the help of the Chenery-Syrquin equations,[12] Mills and Song found:

> The reason that Korea is more urbanized than predicted appears to be that Korea's international sector, and especially its manufactured exports, are much larger than predicted by the Chenery-Syrquin model. Since all international trade ports are in urban areas, it appears that Korea's manufacturing industry is

11. As shown by the United Kingdom, however, even without overall net growth in industrial output or employment some firms or sectors are still growing and can decentralize.

12. Hollis Chenery and Moises Syrquin, *Patterns of Development, 1950-1970* (Oxford: Oxford University Press, 1975).

more concentrated in urban areas, mainly in urban areas with access to ports, than is true in typical developing countries.[13]

An additional factor not mentioned is the very high population density of Korea.

The ability to undertake significant national urbanization policies is strongly affected by the quality of human resources in the country. Both the literacy rate and the percentage of population with more than a high school education constrain what can be undertaken.

Political and Institutional Capacity

Political and institutional constraints are the most important elements of national urbanization policymaking. The selection of an appropriate strategy, the dissemination of information about it, its acceptance throughout the country, and the strength to sustain the strategy over time are decisive factors. There is nothing more harmful to national urbanization strategies than shifting objectives and erratic implementation because they often lead to major irreversible decisions. This affects the growth of the urban system as well as the internal structure of cities. Indicators of the institutional ability to carry out policies are: the degree of ethnic fragmentation, the centralized structure of government, the share of central government expenditures in total public expenditures, and the relative balance between public and private sector investment. The frequency of turnovers in administration is a simple indicator, but the quality of communication between government planners and the business sector is much more difficult to assess.

There are great differences between the urbanization patterns of centrally planned economies and those of market economies, differences which are related to the nature of their growth strategies in agriculture and industry. The context in which both households and businesses choose to locate in certain cities differs substantially between these two types of economy.

A Typology of Countries for National Urbanization Strategies

The three major elements of a national urbanization strategy are: the implicit spatial policies created when formulating national

13. Edwin S. Mills and Byong Nak Song, *Korea's Urbanization and Urban Problems, 1945-1975* (Cambridge, Mass.: Harvard University Press, 1979), p. 42.

economic policies, the appropriate intraurban policies to deal with the problems of the very large cities (particularly congestion and pollution), and the policies to reduce sharp regional disparities and increase the degree of socioeconomic integration of the nation. Given the wide diversity of national conditions among countries, a typology is useful to show the relative emphasis on each of the three elements of a complete national urbanization strategy. Much confusion can be avoided in the comparison of country experiences, and significant results appear to be attainable, if national urbanization strategies and country conditions are more systematically matched.

The simple typology which is proposed covers all the countries of the world because there is much value in contrasting sharply differentiated national spatial situations and in knowing how any given country would be classified in terms of its dominant spatial problems. Then, given a general notion of the national spatial development process in the country compared with that in all the others, the really interesting work of studying its unique traits can begin.

The countries of the world can be grouped into six major groups as long as the major tendencies of each group are considered and the boundaries remain flexible between the groups. First, market and mixed economies on the one hand need to be distinguished from centrally planned economies on the other, because these two different institutional contexts are of major significance for national urbanization strategies and their three components (implicit national policy, intraurban policy for large cities, and interregional policy). Then countries can be distinguished on the basis of their level of development (GNP per capita), their total population, the size of their domestic markets, their population density and their total area, and the presence of very large cities. The six major groups are: (1) very small countries, (2) countries with limited domestic markets, (3) large low-income countries, (4) medium-size, middle-income countries with large cities, (5) advanced industrialized countries, and (6) centrally planned economies; they are presented in table 7. To clarify the content of each group, additional distinctions have been made when useful. The number of countries falling into each category, as well as the averages for the area, the population, the size of GNP, and per capita figures are presented. In addition, the degree of emphasis

Table 7. *Country Typology for National Urbanization Policy*

Country type	Number of countries	Percentage of world population	Land area (thousands of square kilometers)	Group average		
				Total GNP (millions of U.S. dollars)	GNP per capita (U.S. dollars)	Total population (millions)
Market and mixed economies						
1. Small countries						
City-states	2	0.2	1.0	7,853	2,405	3.4
Others[a]	39	0.7	—	—	—	5.8
2. Limited domestic markets	37	5.3	381.7	1,800	354	5.8
3. Large, low income						
South Asia	5	23.1	1,363.4	30,034	158	187.6
Africa	7	5.3	1,360.9	8,148	230	30.6
4. Middle income						
Asia	5	3.7	255.8	17,315	678	30.3
Middle East and Mediterranean	15	5.2	720.7	26,688	2,142	13.9
Latin America[b]	3	1.0	1,234.0	18,251	1,330	13.0
Latin America[c]	6	5.7	2,350.8	42,901	1,145	38.6
5. Advanced economies	19	16.9	1,665.8	219,999	5,890	36.0
6. Centrally planned economies						
China	1	21.3	9,597.0	354,978	410	865.8
Other low income	6	2.2	169.0	4,370	490	14.6
U.S.S.R.	1	6.3	22,402.0	708,492	2,760	256.7
Other middle income	4	1.5	174.5	27,912	1,930	15.6
Higher income	3	1.6	183.0	75,403	3,640	22.0

	Population of the largest city (group average, thousands)	Policies of major significance		
Country type		*National implicit policies*	*Problems of large cities*	*Large regional disparities*
Market and mixed economies				
1. Small countries				
City-states	3,130		x	
Others[a]	—			
2. Limited domestic markets	389	x		x
3. Large, low income				
South Asia	4,500	x	x	x
Africa	2,025	x	x	x
4. Middle income				
Asia	3,496	x	x	
Middle East and Mediterranean	1,840	x		x
Latin America[b]	4,282	x	x	
Latin America[c]	5,484	x	x	x
5. Advanced economies	4,680	x		x
6. Centrally planned economies				
China	10,888			
Other low income	1,063			
U.S.S.R.	7,734			
Other middle income	1,435			
Higher income	1,737			

— Descriptive data not calculated.

Note: Individual country data are presented in Appendix D, table D-5.

a. Includes only members of the United Nations and the World Bank.

b. Latin American countries with population growth rates of less than 2 percent a year.

c. Latin American countries with population growth rates of more than 2 percent a year.

Source: Based on World Bank data.

to be given to each of the three categories of national urbanization policies is suggested in the table.

Small Countries with Market or Mixed Economies

This category includes two subgroups: countries that are very small with populations of less than 2 million and city-states with very small land areas. These countries do not need to have a fully developed, three-dimensional national urbanization strategy. Some have a land area so small that appropriate policies for the distribution of population are mostly a matter of city or metropolitan planning. Among the countries with more than 2 million people, Singapore with 595 square kilometers and Hong Kong with a little more than 1,000 have land areas which are much less than many of the major metropolitan regions of the world. For instance, the Regional Plan Association of New York covers 3,371 square kilometers and many Latin American cities are also bigger.[14] Most of the other countries in this category have populations so dispersed that problems of excessive concentration do not arise; in fact, insufficient levels of urbanization and economically inefficient city sizes may be the problem. While there are more than thirty countries in this category, it represents less than 1 percent of the total world population.

Countries with Limited Domestic Markets

These countries are relatively small in land area, population, and total size of GNP. Because of the limited size of their economy, the potential development of manufacturing industries depends heavily on external markets and on the possibility for regional economic integration. Population concentration in the capital city is difficult to avoid since this is the only location where business firms can benefit from significant economies of scale. There are three major groups in this category: (1) the Central American states which, because of climatic conditions, have a sparse population along the coastal zone, with most urban development on the higher inland plateaus; (2) the Caribbean island economies, in which urban growth is constrained and con-

14. See Gregory K. Ingram and Alan Carroll, "The Spatial Structure of Latin American Cities," World Bank paper presented at the annual meeting of the American Economic Association, August 1978, table 2.

centrated near a few commercial harbors; and (3) the numerous small African states at a low level of development, with a still unstable pattern of urbanization that is heavily dependent on developing a transport network between the capital city and a few small centers. Many of these countries are experiencing a high degree of urban concentration even though their cities are not large at all by international standards. There are thirty-seven countries in this category, representing 5.3 percent of the world population.

Large Low-Income Countries

Among large low-income countries, two continental subgroups are distinguished by marked differences in their institutional, cultural, and economic contexts. First are the low-income countries of South Asia that have extremely large total populations and a significant number of very large cities. The second subgroup consists of the large low-income countries of Africa, which are significantly smaller in size than their South Asia counterparts, but at the same time are quite different in scale from the other countries of the continent. Together these two groups include twelve countries and 28.4 percent of the world population.

Asia. In Asia the large low-income countries are India, Bangladesh, Pakistan, Burma, and, with some significant differences, Indonesia. Their characteristics of urbanization are described here mostly on the basis of the Indian data. These characteristics are unique, and few, if any, of the urban strategies that could be considered in the middle-income countries would make sense in this part of Asia.

These Asian countries, as seen in the case of India, are set apart from other urbanizing countries in several ways. During the third quarter of this century, the rate of population growth in India has been accelerating to produce an enormous growth in both urban and rural populations. The rural sector increased by 63 percent during 1950-75 when the urban sector increased by 121 percent. The level of urbanization, however, has been going up very slowly from about 10 percent at the beginning of the century to only 21 percent in 1975. Although the share of the urban sector has remained relatively stagnant, its absolute size has become very large. In 1975 the urban sector of India represented

Table 8. *India: Distribution of Urban Population by Size of Towns*
(percent)

Census year	100,000 and more	50,000 to 99,999	20,000 to 49,999	10,000 to 19,999	5,000 to 9,999	Less than 5,000
1901	22.9	11.8	16.5	22.1	20.4	6.3
1911	24.2	10.9	17.7	20.5	19.8	6.9
1921	25.3	12.5	16.9	18.9	19.0	7.4
1931	27.4	12.0	18.8	19.0	17.3	5.6
1941	35.4	11.8	17.7	16.3	15.4	3.4
1951	41.8	11.1	16.7	14.0	13.2	3.2
1961	48.4	11.9	18.5	13.0	7.2	1.0
1971	52.4	12.2	17.4	12.0	5.2	0.8

Source: Ashish Bose, "Urbanization in India," in Goldstein and Sly, *Patterns of
Urbanization*, p. 295.

about 9 percent of the world population, and projections indicate
that in the year 2000 it could be as much as 11 percent, for a total
of 355 million.

During the third quarter of the century, rural-to-rural migration has been far more important than rural-to-urban migration.
This rural migration is predominantly over short distances within
the same district. The contribution of rural-urban migration has
been particularly small in India, underlining the stagnation of the
urban sector. Within the urban sector, a reshuffling of the population has occurred through urban-to-urban migration. The percentage of urban population in cities of more than 100,000 has
increased at an accelerated rate, while the share of population in
the small towns of less than 20,000 has been falling steadily, as
shown in table 8. Because of the importance of the rural sector,
table 8 emphasizes the shifts in the size distribution of cities by
using the fairly low cutoff point of 100,000 population for the
largest size. When this urban sector of cities of more than 100,000
is broken into its components, however, another problem is
revealed (see table 9). With the same reservations that apply to
projections for large-scale countries such as China, it is valid to
note that concentration in the largest cities is increasing for India.

Africa. Among the large low-income countries of Africa are
Nigeria, Zaire, Sudan, Ethiopia, Kenya, and Tanzania, to which
could be added Egypt in North Africa. In these countries problems
of imbalances among regions and large population concentration

Table 9. *India: Percentage Distribution of Urban Population for Cities of More than 100,000*

City size (thousands)	1950	1960	1970	1975		2000	
				Percent	Total population (millions)	Percent	Total population (millions)
5,000 or more	0.0	4.5	6.4	5.9	15.0	8.0	73.3
2,000-4,999	9.2	9.7	9.7	10.7	27.5	11.2	103.0
1,000-1,999	14.1	14.0	13.4	13.0	33.4	15.3	140.4
500-999	17.7	16.4	16.7	17.8	45.7	18.5	169.4
200-499	25.9	24.5	24.5	24.2	62.4	22.1	202.8
100-199	33.0	30.8	29.3	28.5	73.3	24.9	209.0
Total urban population (millions)	79.9	122.5	198.8	257.6	257.6	918.1	918.1

Source: United Nations, Population Division, *Trends and Prospects in the Population of Urban Agglomeration, 1950-2000.*

in the capital region are very significant; at the same time, the present level of urbanization is still low (the group average is less than 20 percent). They all have high population growth rates, and the largest cities are among the fastest growing in the world even though they already constitute large urban agglomerations. This group includes seven countries which represent 5.3 percent of the world population.

Middle-Income Countries

Middle-income countries are those most capable of developing very active and comprehensive national urbanization strategies. Their level of urbanization is often relatively high, and their income level indicates that a large volume of resources is devoted to urbanization and deserves much greater planning. All the countries in this group have very large cities, and the quality of their internal policies is a major dimension of their national urbanization strategies. The four geographical subgroups of middle-income countries are those of Asia, those of the Middle East and Mediterranean, Latin American countries with moderate or low urban population growth rates, and Latin American countries with high urban population growth rates.

Middle-income countries are differentiated by the following factors that are important for the formulation of national urbanization strategies:

— Degree of integration of the domestic economy: Low integra-

tion means a low degree of interaction and interdependence
among the regional components of the economy. It is indicated by the presence of large interregional inequalities,
although the entire country has already reached a fairly high
level of development and may have a significant international
trade sector.

— Regional structure of industry—by value of output, by level
of employment, by size distribution of firms, and by form of
organization: A high percentage of manufacturing volume
accounted for by the twenty-five largest firms of the country
indicates the frequency of multiplant, multisectoral organizations which are more responsive to national urbanization
policies; the percentage of manufacturing controlled by the
government implies more scope for spatial policies; and the
distribution of manufacturing output by city is crucial to
urban decentralization policies.

— Degree of centralization of economic power: National
programs of investment in infrastructure are a major component of national urbanization strategy. In addition, labor
and business mobility are affected indirectly and directly by
the ability of local government to provide urban services
efficiently. The extent of control over local expenditures
by the central government has a strong effect on local efficiency.

— The growth rate of the rural population: Whether the rural
population is still growing at a high rate, leveling off, or already declining has a strong impact on the growth of various
cities. In the case of middle-income countries it is particularly
important to determine the dominant migration pattern:
rural-to-rural, rural-to-urban, or urban-to-urban movement.

— Human resources: Middle-income countries are releasing the
constraints on their human resources through education, but
wide differences remain among them in literacy rates and the
proportion of highly educated population.

Asia. There are five middle-income, medium-size economies in
Asia: Thailand, the Philippines, Republic of Korea, Taiwan, and
Malaysia. Though spread apart in their population growth rates
and levels of urbanization, they belong to one of the most dynamic regions of the world and have been shifting their economic
strategies toward manufacturing exports, an approach that will

speed up the pace of their urbanization. Each has been actively reviewing the formulation of its urbanization strategies, and Korea has taken a more comprehensive approach to spatial development, steadily creating new instruments to decentralize away from Seoul.

The needs for a deconcentration of economic activities as a part of an urbanization strategy vary greatly among these five economies. They rank as follows according to the concentration index (table 6):

	Urban concentration	Level of urbanization
Thailand	47	17
Korea, Republic of	45	47
Philippines	28	36
Taiwan	19	64
Malaysia	16	30

Their levels of urbanization vary widely and have no direct relation with urban concentration. Differences can be traced to rural policies, economic growth strategies, and the quality of policies on infrastructure investment. The difference between Korea and Taiwan, which are otherwise very similar in trade policies, social structure, and degree of inequality, is mainly because Korea has a poorly endowed, high-cost agriculture and has switched directly to manufacturing for its development strategy, while rural development has been contributing very effectively to growth in the case of Taiwan. In addition, local governments in Taiwan are financially stronger than those in Korea.[15]

Middle Eastern and Mediterranean countries. In the Middle East the dominant threads of urbanization are geographic contiguity and Islam.[16] In this group are Morocco, Algeria, Tunisia, Libya, the countries of the Arabian peninsula, Israel, Lebanon,

15. For more on growth patterns in the Philippines, Taiwan, Malaysia, and Thailand, see Douglas Paauw and John Fei, *The Transition in Open Dualistic Economies* (New Haven: Yale University Press, 1978). For Korea, see Edward S. Mason, Dwight H. Perkins, Kwang-Suk Kim, David C. Cole, Mahn-Je Kim, and others, *The Economic and Social Modernization of the Republic of Korea* (Cambridge, Mass.: Harvard University Press, 1980).

16. Michael Bonine, "Urban Studies in the Middle East," *Middle-East Studies Association Bulletin*, vol. 10, no. 3 (October 1976); and Janet Abu-Lughod, "Problems and Policy Implications of Middle Eastern Urbanization," *Studies on Development Problems in Selected Countries in the Middle East* (New York: United Nations, 1973).

Syria, Iraq, Turkey, and Iran. These countries have a common historical background but diverging futures. Sudan, which might have been considered within this group, is distinctly different, with a much lower degree of urbanization.

The traditional cities of the Middle East shared a common ideology, structure of society, government, and physical form. It was above all the Islamic religion that dominated personal and family relations, the physical layout of the Middle Eastern city, the mode of government, and the political structure of public life. The long urban traditions of these countries were profoundly affected over the last century by new economic interactions with Western Europe; their self-sufficient economies were opened to colonial interaction with the industrializing European powers and drawn into a new environment of politico-economic relations.

The divergence among the countries of the region is already extremely pronounced. At one end of the spectrum is Israel, a highly urbanized country with a high level of income, whose urbanization policies are dominated by the origins of the state and greatly complicated by disputes with the Arab border states. (It is one very clear example of how state policy, institutional structure, and ideology interact to yield specific patterns of urbanization.) At the other end of the spectrum are Saudi Arabia, Libya, and the two Yemens, which still have a low level of urbanization deeply influenced by geography. But the comparisons end there: Saudi Arabia and Libya are among the richest and the two Yemens among the poorest states of the world. Ideologies concerning the role of the state separate them even more.

In the middle is a group of relatively similar countries which are close to a 50 percent level of urbanization, with intermediate levels of income. With their emphasis on infrastructure and the emergence of a large-scale public sector, major urban functions have tended to gravitate toward a few metropolitan regions. In many of these countries attempts to solve urban housing shortages, overcrowding, and lack of public services have often been confined to strategies to reduce the volume of rural-to-urban migration. But these policies to deflect migration from the largest centers to smaller urban areas do not seem to take proper account of the forces that are generating movements to the capital regions. In some countries (such as Turkey) rural inequalities have been a major factor inducing migration to the cities. In others (such as Libya and Algeria) the acceleration of growth generated by oil or other energy sources has caused resources to be heavily concentrated in a few urban areas. In these countries the water problem is a major constraint on the pattern of urban growth. In addition, rural development programs have been slow to raise rural incomes and increase purchasing power in the hinterland.

Israel as well as the three Mediterranean countries of Spain, Portugal, and Greece are at a higher level of urbanization than the countries of the Middle Eastern group, and their national population growth rates are low to moderate. They have fairly large cities that are growing at a rate of around 2 to 3 percent a year, and their per capita income is high. The urban policies of these countries are influenced by Western European experiences.

Latin American countries with large, rapidly growing cities. Spatial development in Latin American countries is characterized by the contrast between: (1) significant overall development of per capita income, sophistication of the manufacturing sector, and productivity of the economy; and (2) conspicuous structural and institutional barriers to the widespread diffusion of economic and social progress. These countries suffer from significant rural-urban disparities and pronounced differences between large and small cities as well as between regions. The countries with large domestic markets fall into two groups: the middle-income countries with large cities and a rapidly growing urban sector and countries that have already reached a high level of urbanization and have an urban sector that is no longer expanding rapidly.

In the group with large cities and a rapidly expanding urban sector are Mexico, Venezuela, Brazil, Colombia, Peru, and Ecuador. Each shows an urgent need for more appropriate policies and more deliberate attention to every dimension of national urbanization strategies. Their national economic policies have built strong spatial biases into trade protection, credit policies, and treatment of the rural sector. The internal management of cities, particularly of the largest ones, is a major issue; and insufficient socioeconomic integration of the various regions has caused large disparities among them.

Highly urbanized, slowly growing Latin American countries. Chile, Argentina, and Uruguay differ markedly from most other

developing countries because they have reached a high level of
urbanization, and their annual population growth rate is about
one-third that of others in Latin America. These three countries
have run out of many options for the adjustment of their national
urbanization patterns. Most of their policy efforts must be directed toward improving city management policies and assisting
various provinces by promoting the growth of medium-size cities.
In these countries rural-to-urban migration is much less important
than the city-to-city mobility of already urbanized migrants. Thus,
different national urbanization strategies are required that emphasize the system of cities.

Advanced Market Economies

Advanced market economies have reached a stage of urbanization never experienced before. The size of their farm population
has dropped to such a low level that rural-urban migration has
become insignificant. The level of urbanization has reached its
saturation point, but mobility of resources within the urban system is still very important. Depending on the political history of
the country, the degree of centralization of its government, and
its size, two different systems might be observed: a monocentric,
hierarchical system marked by the dominance of the capital
region, or a polycentric system with several important urban centers of more or less the same size playing functionally differentiated roles. Recent analyses of these systems indicate a deconcentration away from the core urban region.[17] The urban movement taking place in countries where rural-urban migration has
exhausted its course could be referred to as mature urbanization,
in contrast to the more familiar situation in which rural-urban
migration plays a major role in shaping the urbanization patterns
jointly with urban-urban migration.

There are major differences between the regional problems of
advanced economies and the diversified range of problems experienced by developing countries, even when the comparison is
limited to the problems of middle-income countries. The advanced economies are highly integrated, and most serious con-

17. Daniel R. Vining and Thomas Kontuly, "Population Dispersal from Major Metropolitan Regions: An International Comparison," *International Regional Science Review*,
vol. 3, no. 1 (1979), pp. 49-73.

straints on the choice of location by private firms have been removed. They are characterized by a well-established civil service, a highly educated labor force, a slowly growing or stationary population, well educated, with a median age above that of developing countries, and a very small degree of dispersion of regional per capita incomes. These advanced market economies are still attempting to make sense out of this new urban context.

National Settlements in Centrally Planned Economies

The urban development process of centrally planned economies does not fit well in any of the four major categories outlined so far. Their rate of urbanization is particularly rapid, but the distribution of the urban population is more even across city sizes than in market economies. Because of the centralized nature of decisions, there is a strong emphasis on matching current needs against the realization of long-term, predetermined goals. These countries appear to be controlling and eliminating extreme fluctuations in the speed of their urbanization. The extensive use of nonmarket decisionmaking has created new ways of affecting factor mobility and urban growth. The most striking difference from market economies is that centrally planned economies have deliberately used their national economic policies to affect urbanization, while market economies too often have ignored these implicit policy instruments.

Centrally planned countries represent almost 33 percent of the world population. Like market economies, they could be subdivided into more homogeneous subgroups: China; other low-income centrally planned economies such as Vietnam, the Lao People's Democratic Republic, and Cambodia; the Soviet Union; high-income centrally planned economies such as Czechoslovakia, the German Democratic Republic, and Poland; and middle-income countries such as Hungary, Bulgaria, and Romania.[18] The two major competing models of national urbanization strategies are the Soviet Union and the People's Republic of China. The general characteristics of the strategies followed by these two countries are discussed further in Appendix B, but a brief out-

18. See Roy E. H. Mellor, *Eastern Europe: A Geography of the Comecon Countries* (New York: Columbia University Press, 1975).

line here can help clarify major differences between centrally planned and market economies.

The most important aspect of the Soviet urbanization strategy has been the systematic attempt to economize on the cost of urbanization and to block rural-urban migration in two ways. Very labor-intensive technologies were encouraged for agriculture, while very capital-intensive technologies were encouraged for industry. This situation encouraged much higher productivity gains in manufacturing than in agriculture. At the same time, the household demand for better urban services, which would have been associated with higher levels of productivity of industrial labor, was suppressed by the absence of a direct link between productivity and wages. Since savings are collected and allocated by the central plan, there has been a tendency to limit the supply of needed urban services. These factors explain why the Soviet Union appears to be controlling the growth of its very large cities better than most other countries. An additional reason has been the emphasis on "new" industrial cities, which has concentrated the supply of new services and skilled labor in intermediate urban centers. Thus the Soviet model combines high rates of urbanization with a very low degree of urban concentration.[19]

Because the People's Republic of China represents more than one-fifth of the world population, its urban policies are of major significance by themselves and as possible models for newly developing countries. Detailed knowledge of urban development in China is still limited. Since 1957 migration to the cities has been drastically reduced by direct controls and the emphasis on rural development. Strict policies have been applied to stop the growth of the three major urban regions: the Shanghai region, the Peking-Tientsin region, and the industrial zones of Manchuria (Harbin, Mukden). The drop in the growth rate of the urban sector, however, has been associated with a similar drop in the rate of industrialization. It remains to be seen whether the abandonment of autarkic development policies and the move toward more de-

19. Gur Ofer, "Economizing on Urbanization in Socialist Countries: Historical Necessity or Socialist Strategies," in *Internal Migration: A Comparative Perspective*, Alan A. Brown and Egon Neuberger, eds. (New York: Academic Press, 1977); and V. G. Davidovich, *Town Planning in Industrial Districts*, translated from the Russian for the National Science Foundation (Springfield, Va.: Clearing House for Federal Scientific and Technical Information, 1968).

centralized economic decisionmaking and international trade will be sustained. A move to a more rapid rate of industrialization would significantly increase the rate of urbanization. The level of urbanization in China so far has been rising faster than in India, even though China is reported to have reduced its population growth rate below 1 percent a year. Like the Soviet Union, China appears to be controlling the growth of the largest cities well. Both the Soviet Union and China, being very large countries, have serious problems of regional inequality.

3

Determinants of the Growth
of Urban Systems

The size of a population, the percentage living in cities, and the
rates of growth of both rural and urban populations in relation to
their level of economic development are all important indicators
of the economic and urban environment in a country. They raise
general expectations about the nature of the cities, the movements
of population, and the kind of transport used or even the housing
system, but they provide only a grossly simplified picture of the
way a country is developing. Aggregate urban indicators may be
enough within the framework of traditional economic theory,
which omits all references to space and treats any economic
activity as if it took place at a single point. At early planning
stages, it may be possible to assume that development analysis
can consist of watching numbers increase at different rates along
two columns, one labeled "urban sector," the other "rural sector."
But when the time arrives to implement policy decisions, the
question "where?" becomes crucial. It will make an essential
difference whether the country is small, like Fiji, or large, like
Brazil; desertic, like Yemen, or regularly drenched by equatorial
rains, like Liberia; flood prone, like Bangladesh, or short of water,
like Mauritania; with wide open plains, like Argentina, or with
valleys divided by mountain ranges, like Colombia; landlocked,
like Zambia, or endowed with a hospitable seacoast, like the
Philippines; within a region of major seismic activities like Iran,
or relatively unaffected by earthquakes. Given a country's existing
urban structure, it matters even more where future investment
should be encouraged.

   In addition to the very specific constraints imposed upon a
country by its physical geography, economic development itself

sets in motion a complex of forces that tend to draw both labor
and capital toward the same regions and to concentrate social and
economic activities in cities, particularly the large ones. Neither
new investment resources nor new additions to the labor force
are spread evenly across a country, nor should they be expected
to be so.

The pattern of industrial investment and the concentration of
population at selective locations have given rise to a debate on a
basic issue of national urbanization strategy. In the formulation of
policies, should the emphasis be on moving capital investment to
the regions where most of the population is currently located?
Or, should migration become the principal means of adjustment
and labor be expected to move where capital investment can be
located most easily? A priori, it would seem preferable to help
existing communities grow and avoid the disruption of losing
their more talented and younger members, who migrate to distant
regions. The earlier analysis has already shown, however, that
such a goal is not easily met and that rural-urban migration is a
major component of urban growth in developing countries.

The decentralization and regionalization of employment are
constrained by the structure of the national and regional urban
system and the way growth impulses are transmitted from city
to city through the mobility of labor, financial flows, the flows
of producer and consumer goods, and the diffusion of innovations. The transport system shapes the national patterns of population settlements for very long periods, but over the medium
term (say, five to ten years) the openings, closings, expansions,
contractions, and moves of business firms play the central role
in the selective growth of cities. At the lower end of the urban
scale, small towns and rural centers interact strongly with the rural
sector and depend on the structure and dynamism of agriculture
for their growth. The policy implications of these elements of
urban growth in developing countries are examined in this chapter.

Urban Systems, City Size, and the Transmission of Economic Growth

In spite of the extreme complexity of urban settlements, only a
few major factors enter into the formulation of national urbanization policy and of particular plans of action for given cities or

urban regions. First and most important, especially for the planning of new economic activities, is that all the cities of a country form an urban system connected by flows of goods, people, and information. This system is constantly evolving and reflects well the stage of economic development and economic integration of a country.[1] In a developing country it is common—and practically a truism—that the poorest provinces have the smallest number of cities in relation to their population, and that, in addition, most of the urban population is concentrated in the main city. In contrast, the richest provinces or states share a much more structured system of cities, quite a few of which will be larger than the capital of the poorest province. This situation could be illustrated by comparing the twenty-two states of Brazil in 1970: the richest state, São Paulo, had sixty-five cities averaging 186,000 people, and the poorest state, Maranhão, had five cities averaging 60,000. The population is concentrated in a few urban centers at the early stages of urbanization and industrialization because economies of scale and the desire to minimize risk and uncertainty favor a few locations.

Analysis of the growth and structure of urban systems leads to the important conclusion that an optimal size for a city is a meaningless planning concept. It is empirically impossible to identify an optimal size for a variety of reasons, stemming from the uncertainty attached to the costs and benefits of urban size. In an analysis of the sources of urban growth it must be emphasized that the size of a city is dependent on its place in the hierarchy of cities in the urban system.

To illustrate the pitfalls of defining some sort of optimal city size without careful attention to the country context: Mexicans feel that Mexico City is much too large with its population of 11.9 million (1976); Koreans feel that Seoul is too large with a population of 7.8 million (1978); Malaysians feel that Kuala Lumpur is too large with its population of 452,000 (1970)—even though Singapore was much larger in 1975 with 2.25 million; and it would not be surprising to hear that Papuans feel that the population of Port Moresby, in Papua New Guinea, with 113,000

1. The term "integration" refers here to the sectoral and geographical mobility of factors of production. It can be extended to the political sphere and related to social mobility.

(1976) is also too large. Part of the problem lies in the distribution of political power and, as previously noted, the difficulty of knowing when a city has reached an optimal size, even when it is the capital city and the linchpin of the entire urban hierarchy.

Clearly, the size of a capital city (or the leading urban center) is related to the size of the national population and the structure of the economy. It is also undeniable that some of the major cities of middle-income countries, such as Seoul, Mexico City, and São Paulo—as in the case of Tokyo two decades earlier—are now reaching population sizes previously attained by Western cities only at a much higher average income level. But the main point to remember is that even these population concentrations are directly related to the structure of the country and the operation of the economy. Any modification of the populations of these cities would change the rest of the urban system. These large concentrations lead to severe problems of traffic congestion and environmental pollution, the solution of which is seriously constrained by the average income level. Proper internal metropolitan policies toward these two problems constitute one of the three major dimensions of national urbanization strategies.[2]

Expanding and Mature Urbanization

The various kinds of urbanization discussed earlier in the world-wide review share many characteristics that define what could be called expanding urbanization. The advanced economies, however, are now entering a phase never experienced before, which could be called mature urbanization. Some of the most important differences between these two types of urbanization are presented in table 10. During the phase of expanding urbanization, industrialization plays a major role, and three successive phases for both can be distinguished: initial concentration, decentralization toward selected locations, and finally a more thorough diffusion of growth throughout the nation.

Mature urbanization is characterized by a reshuffling of urban populations among urban regions, possibly accompanied by further suburbanization of the population within the large metro-

2. As a point of reference, the greater Tokyo region (Tokyo City plus the three prefectures of Saitama, Kanagawa, and Chiba) had 24.1 million residents in 1970 within a fifty-kilometer radius. The average number of daily trips per resident was 2.5 in 1968. See Tokyo Metropolitan Government, *Traffic in Tokyo*, 1975.

Table 10. *Contrast between Expanding and Mature Urbanization*

Item	Expanding urbanization	Mature urbanization
National population	Expanding well above the net reproduction rate. Its average age is young.	Current population growth rates often below the net reproduction rate. The average age of the population is over 30 and a substantial proportion is over 60.
Rural-urban migration	Major force behind the growth of the major cities. Significant factor in the growth of practically all cities of the national urban system. Urban amenities are not a major determinant of migration.	Has practically stopped. The growth of cities is entirely dependent on urban-urban migration. Because migrants are already completely urbanized, they are particularly sensitive to differences among urban amenities. The only factor preventing urban growth from becoming strictly a zero-sum game among cities is international migration.
Degree of economic and social integration	There remain conspicuous constraints to economic and social mobility between sectors as well as geographically.	Most of the constraints on the locational mobility of industry and services have been removed. Amenity-intensive regions have an edge.
Level of income and complexity of the economy	Still not comparable with advanced economies. A major national objective is to reach comparability with advanced countries.	The leading sectors of the economy are intensive in the use of both human capital and information. The majority of the population is employed in the service sector, which has reached high levels of productivity.
Capital region and largest cities	Still growing at a substantial rate.	No longer growing. In fact, there is evidence that the process of deconcentration in the major urban region of the country has already started. Masking this new trend is the important role played by international migration in replacing the larger net out-migration of native urbanites from the capital region.

politan regions. At this stage, city-to-city migration is the dominant factor affecting the system of cities. The determinants of
city-to-city migration are quite different from those of rural-
urban migration: because migrants are fully urbanized, they are
much more sensitive to differences in amenities between cities.
Under conditions of mature urbanization, the core urban regions
are losing jobs and residents to more attractive locations. Both in
Britain and in France decentralization schemes away from Paris
and London have been reviewed and curtailed. In the United
States mature urbanization is leading to regional conflicts between
the Northeast and the Sunbelt, because the gain of one region is
the loss of the other in this new urban environment. Another
common trait of the mature urban countries is that native population losses in the large urban centers are often replaced by foreign immigrants in Paris, London, Stockholm, New York, the
large cities of the Ruhr Valley, and elsewhere.

The contrast between expanding and mature urbanization can
serve as a reminder that there is little reason for middle-income
countries to borrow the strategies currently being followed in
advanced economies, because they are based on different mobility
patterns for labor and businesses. But many of the tools and
techniques used in advanced countries to meet urban problems
deserve careful analysis and can generally be adapted by a middle-
income country for its own national urbanization policies.

Size, Location, and Functions of Cities

The size of a city cannot be evaluated independently of its
location and its function, and it would be convenient to provide
a classification of cities which would be used for the formulation
of urban policies and would be valid for most of the middle-
income countries. There have been, indeed, remarkable efforts to
classify the cities of various countries as well as very substantial
theoretical developments to analyze and explain the structure and
growth of systems of cities. Conceptual models such as central-
place theory, growth-center theory, hierarchical diffusion models,
industrial linkage models, as well as very recent theoretical economic models have considerably improved our understanding of
the economic, social, and political forces affecting urban systems.
At this stage, however, few if any of these analyses have yielded
strong, clear-cut policy results easily transferable from country to

country. They can greatly improve the formulation of national
urbanization strategies, making them more realistic and thus more
effective, but they have yet to yield the convenient recipes, rules
of thumb, and quantitative operational guidelines judged necessary
by decisionmakers.

The immediate empirical outcome of the various theories attempting to provide more precise explanations of the structure
and growth of urban systems has been the classification of the
cities of a country according to their functions and their order of
importance. City classification analysis has a long and sophisti-
cated history, particularly among urban geographers.[3] The objective is to reduce the extreme diversity of city characteristics to a
limited number of major dimensions to improve our grasp of the
urban system. Typical studies analyze more than ninety characteristics of cities for up to 1,100 urban areas. These classifications
have provided better ways of looking at cities, but they cannot
provide unique results uniformly applicable to all policy issues
because the analytical needs of an economist differ from those of
a sociologist, a political scientist, or a physical geographer, even
though urban policymaking eventually requires an interdisciplin-
ary view. These classifications make urbanization policy discussions easier because the position of a city in the urban hierarchy
and its physical location within the country cannot be understood
without knowing its dominant functions. National urbanization
plans will often include detailed descriptions of the important
functions of the cities or regions.[4]

3. The first functional classification scheme is reported to have been done for U.S.
cities by William Ogburn, *Social Characteristics of Cities* (Washington, D.C.: International League of Cities, 1937); there may well exist earlier studies in other countries.
The most frequently quoted pioneering effort is the paper by Chauncy D. Harris, "A
Functional Classification of Cities in the United States," *Geographical Review*, vol. 33,
no. 1 (January 1943), pp. 86-99; it emphasized economic functions and relied on census
data. Since then, numerous studies have been performed for a variety of countries,
frequently in association with the University of Chicago. For references to Canada,
Britain, Yugoslavia, Chile, India, Nigeria, and Ghana, see Brian J. L. Berry, *City Classification Handbook* (New York: John Wiley, 1972), especially chap. 1. An adequate
library search would identify additional case studies of Romania, China, the Netherlands, Japan, Korea, and others.

4. See, for instance, Mexico's Comision Nacional de Desarrollo Urbano, *Plan Nacional de Desarrollo Urbano, 1977-1978,* or the Republic of Korea's *15-year Perspective
Plan, 1979-1991,* chap. 10.

Transmission of Growth and Development among Cities

Classification of cities according to the structure of their economic base provides useful clarification of the growth potential, given the economic orientation of the region and the national economic strategy. It does not, however, provide any insight into the ways in which people, financial funds, producer and consumer goods, and technical and social information move from city to city. Recent work by Pred on the transmission of economic impulses across cities through business networks provides new insights into the structure of urban systems in the case of developed countries.[5] It raises serious doubts about the assumptions made by regional planners in formulating policies for regional development.

The first questionable assumption is that significant investment and increases in the level of economic activity in a city selected as a growth center will generate multiplier effects which will remain concentrated within the target city and its hinterland, defined as its geographical zone of influence. The theory of growth poles is very familiar and has formed the foundation for growth-center policies. Thanks to highly localized backward and forward linkages in the structure of production and to increasing levels of household expenditures, a concentration of investment in well-selected cities is thought to have powerful secondary effects which will substantially expand the local economy and the region. Thus multiplier effects are assumed to be transmitted from cities of a selected size to smaller centers and their surrounding rural areas. This is believed to be especially true for lagging regions, which need to be brought back to levels of performance closer to the national average.

Another conceptual framework that has strongly influenced many policies toward cities is central-place theory. It has been used by geographers in particular to explain the size, function, and sometimes location of cities. The regional concept presented by Christaller was developed with reference to wholesale and retail services and their distribution among cities of different sizes.[6]

5. Alan Pred, *City Systems in Advanced Economies* (New York: John Wiley, 1977).
6. Wilhelm Christaller, *Central Places in Southern Germany*, C. W. Baskin, trans. (Englewood Cliffs, N.J.: Prentice-Hall, 1966).

The smallest size class of rural towns provides the basic high-frequency services needed by the rural hinterland; a fewer number of larger towns provides the smaller towns and the hinterland with more specialized services requiring a larger market. Larger city sizes were associated with services of a higher order and a greater variety of economic activities. This model was found in general harmony with the fact that the size distribution of cities exhibits remarkable statistical regularities from country to country and is very stable over time.

These useful findings related to services have been extrapolated into two unwarranted assumptions. The first one is that what is frequently correct for wholesale and retail services is also true of other types of economic activities, and of the manufacturing sector in particular. The second unwarranted assumption is that economic growth trickles down from major urban centers to the smallest towns throughout the hierarchy of city sizes. More specifically, the deliberate introduction of new economic activities in the largest center of a region is expected to generate further activities through the ranks of the smaller cities. Thus the assumptions are that economic growth is transmitted from larger cities to smaller cities in a predictable way and that upward or lateral interactions are not of great significance to the formulation of policies.

The critique of these theories within the context of the urban system of advanced economies developed by Pred is very useful in itself. For the purpose of this discussion, it has the added benefit of suggesting where and how the urban systems of developing economies tend to differ. Pred is very critical of the propulsive industry version of growth transmission, which has been the foundation of applied growth-pole theory. In his words, "To argue that growth transmission is mostly or fully restricted to the hinterland of a growth center is to maintain that regional or sub-regional city systems have a very high degree of closure, i.e., a low degree of interaction and interdependence with urban units situated elsewhere in the national system."[7]

Many regional planning activities in developing countries are based on weak or unwarranted assumptions concerning the geographic contiguity of a firm's market area to the city where the firm is located and the nature of input-output relations in the

7. Pred, *City Systems*, p. 95.

local economy. They consider neither the nature of industrial organization in the regional economy nor how employment is created, although it matters a great deal whether a firm is a single establishment, a family-controlled or family-managed unit, or a multiplant corporate organization. The problem is that such assumptions ignore the extremely intricate interdependence of the components of the urban systems of advanced economies. They also ignore the "likelihood that a propulsive industrial unit will belong to a multilocational organization with a variety of extraregional, intraorganizational and interorganizational linkages."[8]

The typical technique for appraising the nature of input-output relations has been the construction of input-output tables or their derivatives. Both the simplified models used in developing countries and the few large-scale studies of single regions (Philadelphia, Stockholm, and Seattle) in advanced economies show the large degree of openness of these local economies; many of the most important linkages for goods and services or channels for growth transmission are in nonlocal units. Multiregional input-output models have rarely been built even for advanced economies. The Japanese model built for a set of nine regions shows that the leakages from the poorer regions to the center are particularly important.[9] Other Japanese studies based on regional accounts also show the transfer of earnings from the hinterland to the core region (Tokyo mostly) rather than their local reinvestment within the regional economy. Using simpler methodologies to estimate multipliers, it was found for the new industrial city of Ulsan in the Republic of Korea that the short-run local multiplier was remarkably small. In general, it can be said that the extraregional interdependence of small and less diversified cities will tend to be large if these cities are selected as growth centers.

As Pred points out very effectively, what most distinguishes the urban systems of advanced economies from those of developing countries is the important role played by large organizations in advanced economies. The economies of all developed countries are dominated by large private corporations and government

8. Ibid., p. 96.

9. Takeo Ihara, "Impact Analysis of Interregional Economies: A Tentative Scheme for Development Planning," Pacific Regional Science Conference, East-West Center, Hawaii, 1969.

organizations that are

> multilocational in character, i.e., comprised of a number of
> spatially separated and functionally differentiated units. A
> plentitude of revenue, asset and employment data show that
> the relative and absolute economic might of multilocational
> organizations has burgeoned since the Second World War . . . for
> example, in 1974, 150 business enterprises answered for 88
> percent of Sweden's total export, and partly as a result of
> foreign operations, the country's 200 largest domestically head-
> quartered business organizations had aggregate revenues that
> exceeded the gross national product.[10]

In the case of developing countries, there is no good docu-
mentation of either intraorganizational job control, decisionmaking relations, or sometimes even input-output relations. The
expectation, however, is that the complexity of the structure of
production and its spatial organization will increase with the per
capita income level, the share of manufacturing in total output,
and the size of the banking and financial sector. In the actual
formulation of policies affecting location, a major constraint on
the range of possible actions will be the structure of industry: its
sectoral breakdown and the size distribution of firms within each
sector. I have emphasized the attraction of the largest cities for
most manufacturing activities. The ease with which a firm will be
expanding away from (or even leaving) these cities will be determined by the importance to the firm or to the plants of being
close to a variety of urban services and other enterprises. Large
corporations will be more capable of developing routine operations and providing the necessary support for a branch operation
in a new location. A country's ability to promote large and efficient organizations is a major indicator of its ability to decentralize. In addition, the public sector will play a major role in a country with a significant manufacturing force because public sector
firms can rely on the government to reduce risks.

Implications for National Urbanization Policies

For the formulation of national urbanization policies, a list of

10. Alan Pred, *The Interurban Transmission of Growth in Advanced Economies*,
Research Report no. 76-4 (Laxenburg, Austria: International Institute for Applied
Systems Analysis, 1976), p. 5.

basic propositions can be drawn to guide studies in a given country:

1. The sources of economic growth of a city cannot be inferred from the size of its population; it is dependent on its economic functions and its distance from other urban centers. In particular, cities depending on natural resources (mining, fisheries, tourism, or agriculture) will exhibit growth patterns and potentials quite different from cities of comparable population size performing mostly transport, wholesale, or retail functions.

2. The largest cities of developing countries have an employment structure very similar to that of the major cities in advanced economies. Only a detailed analysis of the structure of their internal labor markets can yield information on specific planning needs and the extent to which dualism prevails. In general, there tends to be a positive relation between diversification, city size, and level of income, given the income elasticity of demand for most urban goods and services.[11]

3. An analysis of Japanese cities done by the Economic Planning Agency in the 1960s supports a general presumption that there tends to be an inverted U curve relating the importance of manufacturing to city size.[12] Beyond a certain level, which varies from country to country, the service sector becomes more important. The findings of this Japanese analysis are generally in concordance with the more recent study of the patterns of employment and industrial structure in the United States done by Bergsman, Greenston, and Healy.[13] In particular, they note that whatever the degree of disaggregation, "the secondary-tertiary distinction remains strong, i.e., manufacturing activities are not closely associated with services, trade, etc." They add that "the

11. For some empirical evidence for a developing country, see Ian Scott, *Urban and Spatial Development: The Mexican Case* (Baltimore, Md.: Johns Hopkins University Press, 1981). For a theoretical interpretation, see Bertrand B. Renaud, "Employment Structure and the Stability of Urban Growth during the Urbanization Process," *Urban Studies*, vol. 13 (October 1976), pp. 292-98; also Joel Bergsman, Peter Greenston, and Robert Healy, "The Agglomeration Process in Urban Growth," *Urban Studies*, vol. 9 (October 1972), pp. 182-205.

12. Miyoei Shinohara, *Structural Changes in Japan's Economic Development*, Economic Research Studies no. 11 (Tokyo: Hitotsubashi University, Kinokuniya Bookstore, 1970).

13. Joel Bergsman, Peter Greenston, and Robert Healy, "A Classification of Economic Activities Based on Location Patterns," *Journal of Urban Economics*, vol. 2 (January 1975), pp. 1-34; and "The Agglomeration Process in Urban Growth."

weakness of positive associations between manufacturing and
services is noteworthy. The few exceptions that suggest actual
linkages are port-related activities and analogous manufacturing,
and pipeline services and oil production and refining."[14]

4. Comparable analyses for developing countries are not available yet, but one main difference can be easily hypothesized:
because of the role played by the income elasticity of demand for
various services, the structure of cities in developing countries
will be less diversified than that of cities of similar population
size in developed countries. Services of the highest order would be
expected to be concentrated in the largest cities of developing
countries, a hypothesis no longer valid in very advanced economies
such as the United States.

5. Classification of cities according to their economic structure
and their sources of growth is very different from their classification according to the needs of the residents. In a developing country the total population and the average income level tend to be
good predictors of the nature of the demand for urban services.
The historical background and the growth rate of the population
are obvious intervening factors. Few, if any, classifications have
ever been based on the structure of local urban services (housing,
urban transport, water supply, and other utilities). While there is
little or no correlation between the population size of a city and
the sources of its growth, there is a much higher correlation between population size and the need for urban services and solu-
tions to the problem. This fact is reflected in the system of local
administration of every country; the urban transport sector is
particularly closely associated with the size and income level of a
city.[15]

In addition to size and economic function, the distance between
cities appears to play a significant role in the growth potential of
the local economy. This hypothesis, which has been given some
preliminary tests, is most clearly stated by Van Boventer: "A
given town has better growth prospects if it is either close by a

14. Bergsman, Greenston, and Healy, "A Classification of Economic Activities,"
pp. 24-25.

15. See, for instance, J. Michael Thomson, *Great Cities of the World and Their
Traffic* (London: Crow-Helms, 1977). The provision of urban services to residents is
discussed by Johannes Linn, *Cities in the Developing World: Policies for Their Equitable and Efficient Growth* (New York: Oxford University Press, forthcoming).

vigorous bigger city or far away from all competing centers, and
there is some intermediate distance at which the town is worse
off."[16] This perception is based on the consideration of two
dominant factors affecting the growth potential of a given urban
center: agglomeration economics and the existence of an economically strong hinterland. The worst location for a small city is a
short distance from a competing center. The farther away from a
competing center a city is, the bigger the potential for further
growth; in that case a rich hinterland will help because the city
would have to be rather big to become fully viable and develop
significant agglomeration economies of its own. Such a useful
insight is, however, difficult to use for actual planning because
there are important intervening factors such as population density,
transport costs, and product as well as factor mobility.

Role of Transport in Shaping Patterns of Settlements

Throughout history, cities have always tended to grow at locations providing significant savings in transport costs: along major
rivers flowing through rich agricultural plains, around seaports,
along navigable lakes, and at the crossroads of major trade routes.
The main effect of modern transport technologies (large-gauge
canals, railroads, modern shipping systems, highway and expressway networks) has been to increase enormously the comparative
advantage of the locations served by these transport systems.

Limited Transport Networks Encourage Urban Concentration

Because the growth of cities now depends heavily on the pace
of industrialization, the most rapidly growing cities are those
located most favorably for economic activities, and the quality of
their transport links becomes an important factor. But economic
forces are not the only source of growth for current urbanization.
Just as in the past, some cities are growing as religious centers
(such as Mecca), military bases, or political centers.

If the structure of the transport network serving a country
affects the pattern of urbanization, it also reacts to it. More new
investment will take place in transport facilities between cities that

---

16. Edwin Von Boventer, "Optimal Spatial Structure and Regional Development,"
Kyklos, vol. 23 (1970), pp. 903-24.

are growing rapidly. In the case of developing countries, the
heritage of a colonial past is often a transport network that fun-
nels goods and services into a major harbor and does not provide
adequate lateral transport between inland regional centers. In
particular, the all-weather road network, instead of covering the
entire country rather evenly, is often tree-shaped and drains all
activities into a trunk line to the main export city connecting the
country to Western markets.

With an inadequate transport network the choice of location is
severely limited, and communications must follow very specific
routes. In Western Europe, North America, or Japan, which have
few transport constraints, the actual road distance between two
significant cities will almost never differ much from the air
distance, the difference being less than 20 or 25 percent. In many
developing countries it is frequently impossible to travel directly
between two relatively close cities, and the only feasible route is
through a fairly distant major city. Urban growth patterns are
therefore deeply affected. In the Republic of Korea, for instance,
the transport policy followed over the last fifteen years has been
to make sure that no place in the country is more than one day's
travel time from any other location. This policy was introduced
at the same time as industrialization and is only now helping deconcentration. In contrast, the fact that Taiwan had an adequate
transport system before in-migration and rapid industrial growth
has been significant for the very balanced distribution of population in Taiwan by world standards.

With the transport networks typical of developing countries,
economic forces tend to accentuate the concentration of economic activities at the transport terminals. On a continental scale,
the way various transport modes have shaped the location and
growth of cities is particularly evident in Latin America.[17] The
major transport systems have often made relations between two
countries easier than between the capital city and its national
hinterland, and former transport patterns continue to affect the
concentration of population along the coast as the strong com-

17. For discussions of other national transport networks, see Brian J. L. Berry,
Essays on Commodity Flows and the Spatial Structure of the Indian Economy, Paper
no. 111, University of Chicago, Department of Geography, 1966; or Peter Haggett,
Locational Analysis in Human Geography (New York: St. Martin's Press, 1966).

parative advantage they initially provided continues to feed further economic growth.

Transport Corridors between Major Urban Centers

A factor of major significance to national spatial development policies is that existing transport corridors between major cities have a tendency to grow stronger over time. In the case of a metropolitan center in isolation, the development of a railroad network or all-weather transport system will favor new and large-scale factories which have comparatively low marginal costs of production because of the size of the market they already serve. Lowered transport costs will further expand the market area that they can profitably serve and will frequently lead to the elimination of smaller-scale producers serving smaller cities in more out-of-the-way locations.[18] With the rapidly increasing output of industry, economies of scale in production and transport tend to expand the market area that can be served from a given manufacturing center and will favor the interdependence of large cities. This trend will be accompanied by greater labor market specialization and the attainment of the minimal size market for specialized products (particularly services) not traded outside major urban centers.

The simplified chain of events leading to more rapid urban growth along the transport link between two major urban centers can be described as follows:

1. The appearance of railroad lines or major highway links (such as the Seoul-Busan expressway in Korea) joining leading urban industrial centers encourages interurban (interregional) trade between the two cities concerned. Because ton-per-mile costs on railroads are typically a function of the total traffic per unit length of track, freight rate economies accrue to the cities at each end, particularly when they have a rapidly expanding traffic in food, supplies, goods in transit, incoming industrial inputs, and

18. Large-scale firms in the richest consumer market have a well-known advantage when new transport systems lower distribution costs. The opening of a better road will suddenly eliminate the natural protection enjoyed by small firms in smaller cities, where traditional crafts will quickly disappear. A typical case is Colombia, which before the improvement of the highway network had provincial urban centers tucked in each valley and serving a limited market.

outgoing manufactured products. The availability of lower freight
rates in relatively few cities along the dominant trunk line helps
attract new manufacturing establishments and stimulates the expansion of existing capacity on site, reducing the competitive
position of less attractive cities distant from the main transport
axis.

2. The growth of traffic between the two cities yields production economies and lowers per unit freight costs. It also improves
the diffusion of labor market information for the migrant labor
force in favor of these dominant cities.

3. The growth of traffic offers the opportunity to reduce shipping rates or to improve transport services, which further stimulates interurban trade. A larger volume of trade will permit major
investment in new facilities: for railroads, double-tracks, electri-
fied lines, faster locomotives, more frequent runs; for road transport, large-scale container facilities and truck service stations. Such
services will come first to the major urban centers at each end of
the transport axis.

4. With rapid growth, increasing congestion and the rising cost
of nontraded services in the major centers will induce new industries to locate away from the two major urban centers. The
best location will be in a smaller city along the main transport
axis, at a secondary transport node with easy access to the two
major markets and quality transport services.

Relations between a City and Its Hinterland

The effect of increasing transport efficiency between two major
centers can be contrasted with the dynamic impact of rural roads.
Transport between two major centers promotes the rapid growth
of economic activities along the trunk line more than elsewhere
in the country and concentrates economic activities in the two
centers. Transport in rural areas opens up new areas to profitable
agricultural development, often increasing agricultural productivity and output as well as stimulating migration. For the purpose of
making investment decisions, the two types of transport differ in
the traffic that is expected to materialize with the reduction in
costs: to the projected growth of traffic (which transport economists distinguish as "normal") must be added the growth induced
by lowered costs ("generated" traffic). In other words, in a major
corridor investment follows the demand for transport, while in

rural areas investment in transport is expected greatly to stimulate economic growth and lead to much higher levels of future traffic.[19]

The projected change in the use of a rural road is critically dependent on the answer to several basic questions:

— Who benefits from the saving in transport costs created by the new road? Is the impact evenly spread among producers, traders, and consumers?
— What will be the response of producers to higher farm prices, lower input costs, and higher quality of service, particularly greater frequency and improved reliability? Will savings be enough to induce a measurable increase in inputs? Will lower transport costs permit the introduction of significantly new inputs?
— Will the improvement in transport lead to entirely different market structures for farm inputs which will favor the local import of goods not previously available? Will migration be accelerated?

There is no way to predict the distribution of the costs and benefits of new transport investment among producers and consumers or the pattern of interaction between small urban centers and their hinterland. For instance, in Iran, Colombia, and Brazil the benefits of better rural-urban integration through improved transport were absorbed mostly by urban-based intermediaries who captured a large proportion of the cost savings without meaningful improvement in the incentives to the producers.[20] In two cases the benefits were absorbed by the market middlemen who collect and transport the product; in Brazil the lion's share was absorbed by the transport companies. The structure of farm production also has an effect on rural-urban interaction. Land tenure and the agricultural credit system may concentrate benefits to land-owning farmers or absentee landowners and bypass tenants. A World Bank evaluation of a rural road project in Madagascar (Andapa Basin), however, found the road and improved access to markets and other services beneficial to producers. After ac-

19. Curt Carnemark, Jaime Biderman, and David Bovet, *The Economic Analysis of Rural Road Projects*, World Bank Staff Working Paper no. 241 (Washington, D.C., 1976).
20. Ibid., p. 12.

counting for the effects of price controls both on the price of crops (vanilla, coffee, and rice) and on transport tariffs, the study found that roads significantly improved the potential of the region. This finding is consistent with the fact that the crops considered, particularly rice, were "transport intensive," that is, a large proportion of the delivered price on consumer markets was due to transport costs.

In general, one cannot expect that new rural-urban transport links will lead to major producer responses. The effect of new transport investment is often limited to the release of constraints on the expansion of existing economic activities. The direct effect of investment on local output depends on the degree to which local commodities are transport intensive. The more transport-intensive the local commodities, the more elastic the derived demand for transport. In all cases rural roads should benefit rural centers and small towns.

Policy Implications

Given the existing network of cities and the associated transport system, a national urbanization policy needs to build on the existing strengths of the system and to emphasize intermediate cities of substantial size (which will vary for each country) located in the major urban corridors. Even within such corridors, there will frequently be a wide choice among major locations. There is a very low probability that decentralization can be accomplished by providing major central government support to growth in the relatively isolated capital city of a low-income province, particularly when that province has not yet reached a significant level of manufacturing and related economic activities. Prematurely forcing major manufacturing activities into such locations can prove costly to the national economy and fatal or nearly fatal to the firm (as when Asia Motors moved to Gwangju, South Cholla, Korea, in 1968). The general timing of investment in such stagnant or slowly growing regions must be with reference to the pace of growth of other regions and the overall long-term outlook for the national economy.

In most developing countries the development of economic activities along the major transport corridors should be encouraged, not discouraged. The possibility for the spread of manufacturing activities will also be related to the opening of new transport links with the main corridors. As discussed further on, however, new transport links with self-contained "new towns" are likely to be the most expensive and least effective way of attempting decentralization.

It would be greatly misleading to argue that the growth of cities is entirely determined by historical and current patterns of intercity transport investment. The relatively undeveloped transport system of developing countries plays a major role in the rapid growth of larger cities because it provides them with a major economic advantage over other locations. But that does not mean that industry does or should select a location merely to minimize transport costs. The expansion of the transport system over time will relax constraints on alternative locations. In addition, other constraints on the location of economic activities progressively farther from major centers also need to be released because the development of modern cities is determined by the growth of employment and labor mobility.

Role of Industrialization in the Concentration of Population

In the formulation of national spatial development policies, a sound understanding of the factors affecting business mobility is more important than the understanding of the determinants of migration because, fundamentally, migrants have to go where the jobs are. In particular, a realistic understanding of the location of manufacturing activities is central to the understanding of the growth of cities and the organization of economic activities in space.

Why Single Out Manufacturing Activities?

There are three major reasons for singling out the location of manufacturing employment as a major element in designing and implementing spatial, social, and land-use policies at the national and the regional level, even though manufacturing employment seldom constitutes the largest source of employment in the capital region of a country (see table 11 reporting the employment structure in eight cases). First, although the service sector plays a very important role in the cities of developing and advanced economies alike, most services are still consumer-oriented and thus closely tied to the population of the cities. These population-

Table 11. *Occupational Structure of Selected Capital Cities*
(percent)

Sector	Seoul[a] (1970)	Kuala Lumpur[b] (1970)	Manila[c] (1970)	Abidjan[d] (1970)	Tunis[e] (1972)	U.S. metropolitan labor markets[f] (1960)		Bogotá[g] (1972)
						Small	Large	
Agriculture and mining	2.3	7.0	3.5	4.6	1.8	7.1	1.0	1.0
Manufacturing	22.7	20.5	22.1	22.5	18.9	25.1	30.2	28.5
Construction	7.1	6.0	6.5	10.4	5.9	6.0	4.8	9.5
Transport	4.3	6.6	9.7	10.1	6.0	3.9	4.6	12.1
Commerce	28.9	17.6	13.8	18.6	17.5	28.4	32.6	23.5
Public utilities	1.5	1.4	0.8	1.0	1.4	1.4	1.3	n.a.
Services	33.0	35.5	37.3	42.8	39.2	28.8	24.8	30.8
Others	n.a.	5.3	6.2	n.a.	9.3	3.1	5.3	2.2

n.a. Not available.

Note: Columns may not add to 100 because of rounding.

a. Seoul Metropolitan Government, *Seoul Statistical Yearbook, 1971.*

b. World Employment Program, International Labour Organisation (WEP-ILO), "Urbanization and Employment in Kuala Lumpur" (Geneva, February 1975).

c. World Bank data.

d. WEP-ILO, "Urbanization and Employment in Abidjan" (Geneva, 1974).

e. World Bank data.

f. Thomas M. Stanback and Richard V. Knight, *The Metropolitan Economy* (New York: Columbia University Press, 1970).

g. World Bank-UNDP, Bogotá Urban Development Study (Bogotá, September 1973).

serving activities are not greatly amenable to locational control at the national and regional level although they are influenced by internal metropolitan planning. In addition, these activities do not generate much income outside the city they serve. A second reason is that manufacturing firms are much more mobile than firms in the service sector. Studies of the service industries in advanced economies have shown that even relatively mobile service firms are less important than manufacturing in terms of the volume of movements (number of firms and jobs), the distance of the move, and the range of new locations selected.[21] The third and most important reason for concentrating on the location of manufacturing employment is that it is most likely to have a greater multiplier effect on the local and regional economy than a similar employment expansion in the service sector.

Opening, Closing, and Relocation of Firms

Several countries have announced policies to encourage the dispersion of manufacturing activities away from the capital region. In fact, incentives toward decentralization of manufacturing activities are often the cornerstone of explicit national urbanization strategies. These are designed on the basis of weak empirical knowledge: remarkably little is known in developing countries about the sources of change in the composition of the manufacturing sector in major cities.

At present only broad impressions of the likely level of manufacturing mobility can be derived from comparison of annual investment data at the national level with the available data on manufacturing employment by city. In a stagnant economy, where the volume of manufacturing investment is low, one would not expect many opportunities for spontaneous decentralization because most firms are operating below capacity. For any period, much of the investment in manufacturing will be to replace equipment or expand existing facilities.

Detailed information on the movement of industry affecting large cities, particularly in developing countries, is very scarce and

21. Interested readers can refer to Council of Planning Librarians, *Office Location: An International Bibliography* (Madison, Wis., 1977), and the earlier bibliographies provided by the Location of Offices Bureau, an office of the U.K. government, which has been a major instigator of office location analyses in Great Britain, 1972 and 1975.

Table 12. *Manufacturing Firm Size and Employment Distribution: Comparison of Bogotá and Cali with U.S. Cities*

Firm size (number of employees)	Bogotá		Cali		Washington, D.C.	
	Percent	Cumulative percent	Percent	Cumulative percent	Percent	Cumulative percent
	Firm size distribution[a]					
Less than 20[b]	57.55	57.55	55.25	55.25	59.11	59.11
20-49	24.17	81.72	22.45	77.70	24.53	83.64
50-99	10.11	91.83	11.95	89.65	8.88	92.52
100-499	7.43	99.26	9.33	98.98	6.54	99.06
500 or more	0.75	100.00	1.02	100.00	0.93	100.00
	Employment distribution[a]					
Less than 20[b]	14.25	14.25	10.78	10.78	12.17	12.17
20-49	18.26	32.51	12.71	23.49	17.47	29.64
50-99	17.31	49.82	15.79	39.28	13.63	43.27
100-499	35.74	85.56	36.32	75.60	31.20	74.47
500 or more	14.45	100.00	24.39	100.00	25.54	100.00
	Average firm size (persons, cumulative)					
Less than 20		9.95		10.07		9.07
20-49		30.35		29.21		31.35
50-99		64.80		68.12		67.61
100-499		193.34		200.81		210.00
500 or more		771.63		1,233.00		1,203.50
Average		40.18		51.58		44.04
Thousands of persons						
Population[c]		3,453		1,057		2,862
Total employment[c]		1,157		351		1,110
Manufacturing employment[c]		291		106		67
Manufacturing employment share (percent)		25.16		30.20		6.04

a. Figures are for 1970 for Bogotá and Cali; and 1973 for U.S. cities. All U.S. figures are for the central city.

b. For Bogotá and Cali, this category cover 5-19; and for U.S. cities, 4-19.

c. The 1977 estimate for the Special District of Bogotá and Cali, the 1970 U.S. census figures for U.S. Standard Metropolitan Statistical Areas.

does not tell much about the distances of moves across metropolitan boundaries. The typical accounting procedure for tracing industrial movements requires the decomposition of the net changes in the number of firms and the size of employment into openings of new firms, closings of firms, expansion *in situ*, decline *in situ*, and actual moves across city boundaries. Preliminary findings of an analysis of the Bogotá industrial directory indicate that the level of relocation within the capital region is substantial and affected more than 5 percent of the firms annually from 1970 to 1975. But preliminary results from the survey indicate that

	Boston		Chicago		Los Angeles	
	Percent	Cumulative percent	Percent	Cumulative percent	Percent	Cumulative percent
Firm size distribution[a]						
	50.39	50.39	46,89	46.89	53.03	53.03
	25.08	75.47	24.06	70.95	24.48	77.51
	12.93	88.40	11.60	82.55	11.18	88.69
	10.95	98.45	14.61	97.16	9.84	98.53
	1.56	100.00	2.84	100.00	1.46	100.00
Employment distribution[a]						
	7.57	7.57	4.95	4.95	8.07	8.07
	12.28	19.85	8.37	13.32	13.48	21.55
	13.92	33.77	9.00	22.32	12.40	33.95
	31.15	64.92	33.42	55.74	30.79	64.74
	35.08	100.00	44.26	100.00	35.25	100.00
Average firm size (persons, cumulative)						
		9.78		9.60		9.53
		31.86		31.57		34.48
		70.05		70.46		69.47
		201.78		207.66		195.87
		1,465.40		1,416.58		1,509.07
		65.07		90.80		62.62
		2,754		6,978		7,041
		1,098		2,503		2,596
		262		782		719
		23.87		31.20		27.70

Source: Kyu-Sik Lee, "Intra-Urban Location of Manufacturing Employment in Colombia," World Bank paper presented at the annual meeting of the American Economic Association, August 1978; revised August 1979. Figures for U.S. cities are from Gregory K. Ingram, "Reductions in Auto Use from Carpools and Improved Transit," Harvard University, October, 1976; they are derived from *County Business Patterns*, 1973, and data on journey to work (table 2) of the 1970 U.S. census.

only a small fraction of the openings (8.8 percent of the firms, 5.7 percent of jobs) have come from interregional moves. The rate of closings has been smaller, and there is no information on decentralization decisions. The comparative results for Bogotá, Cali, and five U.S. cities show that both the manufacturing structure and mobility patterns do not differ dramatically between Colombia and the United States (see tables 12 and 13).

Preliminary impressions from the ongoing study of Bogotá suggest a continuous and significant amount of internal relocation of manufacturing activities within the metropolitan region and a

Table 13. *Opening, Closing and Relocation Rates of Firms in Bogotá, Cali, and U.S. Cities*

City	Openings				Closings				Relocations			
	Firms		Employment		Firms		Employment		Firms		Employment	
	Percent of base	Annual rate	Percent of base	Annual rate	Percent of base	Annual rate	Percent of base	Annual rate	Percent of base	Annual rate	Percent of base	Annual rate
Cleveland[a]	9.97	3.22	2.59	0.86	14.07	4.49	7.75	2.52	13.83	4.41	5.77	1.89
Minneapolis-St. Paul[a]	12.29	3.94	6.17	2.02	18.00	5.67	11.25	3.62	15.93	5.05	8.28	2.69
Boston[a]	6.10	1.99	1.30	0.43	13.40	4.28	8.00	2.60	9.80	3.17	4.70	1.54
Phoenix[a]	24.40	7.55	12.10	3.88	20.20	6.32	5.30	1.74	8.90	2.88	4.70	1.54
New York[b]	10.21	4.98	3.95	1.96	7.56	3.71	3.55	1.76	11.45	5.57	1.24	0.62
Bogotá[c]	52.38	8.79	31.96	5.70	27.01	4.90	12.61	2.40	19.12	3.56	16.59	3.12
Cali[c]	43.13	7.44	24.48	4.48	26.88	4.88	11.27	2.16	18.33	3.42	10.40	2.00

a. From Raymond Struyk and Franklin James, *Intrametropolitan Employment Location* (Lexington, Mass.: D. C. Heath, Lexington Books, 1975); covered 1965-68 period (1965 was the base year).

b. From Robert Leone, *Location of Manufacturing Activity in the New York Metropolitan Area*, Ph.D. dissertation, Yale University, 1971; covered 1967-69 period (1967 was the base year).

c. The period covered was 1970-75; 1970 was used as the base year. The base year figures can be seen in Kyu-Sik Lee, "Distribution of Manufacturing Establishments and Employment in Bogotá and Cali," City Study Workshop Paper, World Bank, Washington, D.C., 1978. In the case of Bogotá, the relocation figures include establishments that moved at least to another *sección* (a subdivision of a barrio); in the case of Cali the figures include establishments that moved at least to another barrio. Including the moves within the same section, the annual relocation rate of establishments was 5.12 percent for Bogotá and 4.28 percent for Cali.

Source: Lee, "Intra-Urban Location of Manufacturing Employment in Colombia."

much smaller amount of intercity movement, particularly out of the region. This weak outward relocation flow is confirmed by the analysis of changes in industrial employment by city size.[22]

Relocation Decisions

The existing industrial location theory is rather ill adapted to policy formulation in developing countries because it assumes rationality, complete information, and a set of static conditions and disregards the regional, national, and international economic context by taking it completely as given. In reality, location decisions are made in a context of very incomplete information. The entrepreneur, whether the manager of a large-scale textile plant or the operator of a food store, must consider a wide variety of factors which are imperfectly known, or totally unknown, and then decide whether the business can be expected to adjust to them, to survive and prosper. The uneven access to information and its unreliability are major reasons for the spatial concentration of economic activities at the early stages of development.

In formulating policies for industrial dispersal, it is important to keep in mind that the choice of a new location for manufacturing investment presents unique problems to the manager of the organization, whether it is a public or a private corporation. Except in the case of extremely rapidly growing economies, it is a decision which businesses face very rarely. Even for a business of a significant size, an individual manager is not likely to go through this experience more than a couple of times in his entire career. In developed and developing countries alike, the majority of firms have few precedents, no solid rule of thumb, and no record of past experience on which to rely. The range of factors to be analyzed is extremely wide, and even for the same type of manufacturing activities, the factors that are really binding can vary significantly from case to case. And a bad decision will be difficult to reverse.

The fact that the location decision is a limited search process helps explain the distribution of economic activities in advanced economies and developing countries alike. To understand why rapid industrialization in the early stages of development favors concentration of economic activities in the largest cities, it is

22. See Linn, *Cities in the Developing World.*

necessary to take a closer look at the steps in deciding on a business location. All research on industrial mobility indicates that the relocation decision could have been improved with more planning and forethought and that the quality of the search process is closely related to the importance of the business and the size of the operation involved.[23]

The reason business managers are always short of experience in making a location decision is that it is a discrete and unique step. In small firms it is a very infrequent decision; in large firms, although more moves might be made, there is seldom a justification for a specialized team within the organization, even in advanced economies. For these reasons, specialized expertise on location search is hardly expected in developing countries.

Managers must first decide whether a move is really needed or whether there are better alternatives. Depending on size, they must decide between making a complete transfer and opening a branch plant; they must decide on the timing and the scale of the new operation and on the search procedures. In choosing a location they must consider transport and communications, ties with other company operations, labor conditions (such as the availability and quality of labor, the existence of unions, and training requirements), supplies of materials and components, access to services, central and local government services, and amenities. Once this stage has been reached, a site must be chosen on the basis of intraurban location, physical characteristics, tenure, availability of buildings, access to services, and price. Then follows the transition into a new plant with its own series of problems and, finally, the period when operations are starting, but full production efficiency and viability have yet to be reached.

The multitude of problems which must somehow be solved if a business operation is to operate profitably and successfully makes the largest cities almost irresistibly attractive to a businessman whose location decision is consciously made and who has actually considered alternative cities. It also explains why the largest cities are the most likely places to begin activities that are new to the country.

---

23. For one of the most thorough reviews of the problems confronting a manager, see Peter M. Townroe, *Planning Industrial Location* (London: Leonard Hill Books, 1976).

The lack of economic integration, that is, the lack of geographic and sectoral mobility of factors of production, is by itself a factor in location. The less developed the economy, the greater the likelihood of location at the only large urban center and the polarization of economic activity. One of the lasting findings of classical location theory is the distinction between economic activities that are market-oriented and those oriented toward raw materials and resources. The general rule is that the best location for an activity pulled between its major market and its major source of supply is seldom, if ever, the intermediate location: either the market or the supply source must be preferred. Thus, except for mining and transport-intensive activities, the major cities would be preferred because they have the greatest concentration of income and population. The average per capita income of the capital is typically 40 to 60 percent higher than the national figure, and a high proportion of the national population is concentrated within a thirty-five-kilometer radius.

Branch Plants in Provincial Cities

A central argument in favor of the dispersion of manufacturing activities has been the two-stage effects of locating a new industry in a region. In the short run, it is said, the new manufacturing facility will contribute to raising local incomes and to reducing the level of unemployment. In the long run, these same firms are expected to generate secondary development with "new plants forming *short* backward linkages with other local firms and introducing new concepts and ideas to indigenous entrepreneurs and thereby stimulating diversification and growth."[24] Underlying this argument is the expectation that any region which lags behind, either in technological knowledge or rate of adoption of new techniques, can expect, in the long run, to grow more slowly than other regions.

Most of the studies of the spatial diffusion of innovation through the decentralization of manufacturing firms deal with the experience of more advanced economies such as the United Kingdom, Sweden, the United States, and France. Most of the plants that have been located in outlying areas have been branches

24. A. T. Thwaites, "Technological Change, Mobile Plants and Regional Development," *Regional Studies*, vol. 12, no. 4 (1978), pp. 445-62.

of firms, the results of growth which could not be accommodated by existing facilities in the metropolitan center.[25] They have increased local employment and contributed to the diversification of the local industrial structure. But they have not contributed to the diffusion of innovation within the region. Typically, branch plants mass produce relatively standard goods, and large firms are "unlikely to decentralize anything to branch plants that require day-to-day supervision from head office, and this results in routine production at sites distant from the corporate or research center."[26]

Some diffusion of innovation could take place between the new facility and indigenous units through linkages created by purchases and sales. But, in general, the record shows that a wide variety of short-distance local linkages seldom evolves. Branch plants controlled from headquarters appear slow to change suppliers, and because of their low volume of orders to local suppliers, their presence does not lead to higher levels of technological sophistication and performance among purely indigenous firms. Unless specific policies are used to improve links with other regional firms, it is not at all certain that the new firms will diffuse their own knowledge locally or learn from their local environment and modify their own production methods.

A method frequently advocated to attract new manufacturing plants to provincial cities is the organization of industrial estates. These estates can be an excellent urban planning technique at the city level for the rapid provision of land and services, particularly in countries with scarce industrial land. But they are neither necessary nor sufficient to attract industry to a provincial location. They can be a heavy burden on a local government if they are too large or premature. Most successful industrial estates are either export-processing zones or free-trade zones in the capital region or in major harbors. Their success has been quite directly related to the country's overall strategy for industrial development and the policy climate. In the Republic of Korea, which has one of the most successful programs of manufacturing for export, 80

25. See David Keeble, *Industrial Location and Planning in the United Kingdom* (London: Methuen, 1976); and Peter M. Townroe, "Branch Plants and Regional Development," *Town Planning Review*, vol. 46, no. 1 (1975), pp. 47-62.
26. Thwaites, "Technological Change."

percent of manufacturing employment was provided outside the industrial estates.

In the case of domestic-oriented industrial estates, success can be quite elusive. There has been a significant contrast between the inland industrial estates of Korea, which were expected to serve the domestic markets, and the export-oriented estates (which were not all free-trade zones). The inland estates have progressed at a much slower pace, remained underutilized for long periods, and have had difficulty integrating backward with local or national firms. It is only recently that the prospect for such industrial estates has improved with the sustained rapid growth of the Korean manufacturing sector, the overall scarcity of industrial land in the country, and the newly found strength of the domestic market (the Korean per capita GNP was US$300 when the local industrial estate program was initiated in 1968; by 1978 it had risen to US$1,200).

More important than industrial estates in stimulating the growth of regional centers are government policies which will raise the quality of the human capital in the regions through educational programs, technical schools, and national technical and industrial research organizations with branches in every significant center. Cofinancing by government and private industry of technical high schools and universities is an important means of diffusing innovations at the regional level. The capacity to organize and the ability to circulate information rapidly are crucial to the vitality of a region. The growth of regional information networks must be actively encouraged.

Constraints on Decentralization

The various reasons there are so few obviously good locations in developing countries are summed up here, together with some of the major factors which deserve special attention if decentralization and population deconcentration are to be achieved rapidly.

1. The transport system of the country may be insufficiently developed and serve only a few major locations effectively. In addition, the quality of the network may be such that the time cost of shipping even over relatively short distances can be a serious burden.

2. Reliable information about provincial locations is often difficult or impossible to obtain. "There is frequently the possibility that something that has been taken for granted will not be available and that the firm will be put to the expense and waste of energy of going into these activities to supply it itself." This is what Alonso called "diseconomies of internalization."[27]

3. A certain minimal size and level of income is required for the operation of important facilities such as airports, transport terminals, and other major infrastructure. But more important, a minimal size is necessary for the profitable operation of specialized business services, shippers and jobbers, financial offices, legal offices, trade associations and newsletters, repair services, specialized printing facilities, consulting services, equipment leasing, laboratories, and professional schools. These services, much more than the availability of cheap labor, define the attractiveness and the healthiness of a city for a business firm. (See figure 4, where the great differences in levels of services among Korean cities are shown for 1968-70, just when the Korean economy was beginning to take off. Moreover, this indicator does not reflect the quality of the services.)

4. A large urban market reduces the need for a firm to hoard labor and resources in order to meet unexpected problems such as spoilage or unexpected orders. In particular, a large pool of skilled labor greatly facilitates the operation of a firm. A low rate of unemployment in a large city provides a greater reserve of labor than would a higher rate of unemployment in a smaller center. When a new firm locates in a developing country's smaller center, a large proportion of its skilled manpower will have to be brought from the larger cities until on-the-job learning progresses sufficiently.

5. A large pool of skilled labor is also an advantage in the case of suppliers of other inputs, repairs, and services. The probabilistic advantages of urban size are well known: uncertainty, when spread over larger numbers, is more predictable and therefore less risky. This explains the strong correlation between the number of functions and the size of a city.

27. William Alonso, *Industrial Location and Regional Policy in Economic Development*, Center for Planning and Development Research Working Paper no. 74 (Berkeley: Institute of Urban and Regional Development, University of California, 1968).

Figure 4. Indicator of Level of Services in the Republic of Korea
by City or Group of Cities, 1968-70

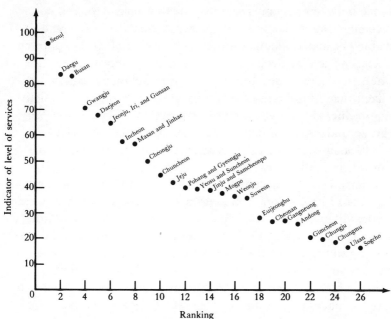

Note: The indicator is based on four types of equipment and services: the number of wholesale commodities available, the number of professions represented, the type of public facilities, and the number of educational subjects taught in the schools.

Source: OTAM-Metra, international consulting firm, 1971.

6. The large scale of cities offers pecuniary externalities to the firms. The large scale of operations for suppliers allows smaller costs and more convenient services, which in turn improve the operations of other firms. This also explains why certain cities tend to become particularly dynamic in selected industrial fields.[28]

7. Face-to-face contacts and social forces are extremely strong in developing countries. They push toward spatial concentration and affect the operation of businesses of all sizes for several

28. The most complete analysis of this agglomeration process was done for the United States, using 186 activities and 203 Standard Metropolitan Statistical Areas in 1971. See Joel Bergsman and others, "A Classification of Economic Activities Based on Location Patterns," *Journal of Urban Economics*, vol. 2, no. 1 (January 1975), pp. 1-34.

obvious reasons. First, communication systems are poorly developed, telephone and other systems are deficient, and the physical distance between persons is a much greater barrier than in advanced economies. Second, technical information is not readily available because trade magazines, technical catalogs, government publications, and a specialized press are in limited supply. Third, business practices in developing countries are much less standardized than in industrialized nations: terms of contracts, deliveries, product specifications, and a variety of practices do not follow set patterns and depend far more on direct verbal communication and personal supervision. Fourth, the structure of business is much less organized or standardized: sustained, frequent personal relations are a more significant part of the conduct of business. Fifth, business managers in developing countries are much less likely to consider their staff as a perfectly standardized and substitutable unit of labor, expected to produce certain results according to some set schedule. Personal and human commitments are an essential dimension of the conduct of business. Professional advancement is strongly influenced by personal networks and patronage by more senior staff. This leads to a concentration of entrepreneurial talent in the capital region and a profound reluctance to relocate in the provinces.

8. In addition to its advantages for business operations, the capital city is extremely attractive in every developing country because intellectual, business, cultural, religious, and political elites interact and overlap more than in large industrialized countries. Location in a small provincial town is considered as an exile and a threat to the future success of one's children. Such an attitude on the part of staff and managers alike is an additional restriction on the location search.[29] Family businesses in particular will not branch out to regional centers very easily. Reliance on family members will often limit the potential growth of a business because continuing expansion will strain the managerial skills of the family and require opening the firm to outsiders.

29. In Korea in the 1970s, which was in a transitional phase of spatial development, a striking percentage of managers worked in the provinces, staying at bachelor's quarters during the week and returning to Seoul to see their family at regular intervals, so as to maximize the educational opportunities of their children and their future professional chances. Such arrangements are feasible because of the greatly improved transport system and may be a way of improving the availability of engineering and managerial talent currently in great demand.

The constraints on the choice of location described above for the manufacturing sector apply equally well to small-scale firms and self-employed workers. The main difference lies in the fact that small businesses and services cater to either larger firms or the consumption needs of the city population and are therefore dependent economic activities. The locational difficulties for this second group are related not to the choice of city, since small-scale activities are more or less bound to their present region, but rather to the choice of neighborhood and actual site in the city. This is why the structure of a normally operating city will tend to be differentiated spontaneously, irrespective of zoning practices, into clusters of similar and complementary activities with specialized neighborhoods of urban trades so familiar to the urban planner: retail trade, wholesale trade, and automobile parts. The distribution of employment in the capital region of a middle-income country forms a highly structured pattern which changes over time in a manner comparable to that in Western European or North American cities.[30]

Migration

In formulating national spatial development policies, planners and analysts tend to consider the migration of labor a more important problem than economic flows of business and capital resources; paradoxically, the opposite is true. Too much has been made of the attraction of city lights for young rural migrants and the notion that improving housing will accelerate migration or, worse, that the removal of squatter settlements and low-quality housing with limited urban amenities will deter migration.

The Job Search

All studies of migration are unanimous in agreeing that long-term migration is perfectly rational: migrants will go where the jobs and the opportunities are and where they will improve their living conditions. As long as the barriers of time, distance, cost, and information are high, rural migrants might settle down in

---

30. For a precise description for Bogotá, Colombia, see Lee, "Intra-Urban Location of Manufacturing in Colombia"; and for general analysis, see Byung Nak Song, "The Distribution and Movement of Jobs and Industry: The Seoul Metropolitan Region," Korean Development Institute Working Paper no. 7411 (Seoul, 1974).

small and medium-size cities. But as soon as transport barriers are lowered, the more traditional small-scale, high-cost businesses of small cities will no longer be protected, the capital region will become more accessible, and the flow of migrants to the capital will promptly swell (as, for instance, in the case of Colombia). If it happens that the economy is also booming, massive migration to the capital city will take place at an alarming rate, as was the case in Korea in 1965-70 (when Seoul grew at 9.3 percent a year) or in São Paulo during the same period.[31]

If the creation of employment triggers mobility and induces migration, there is also a secondary employment effect created by the growth of the population coming from migration, which raises further the demand for nontraded goods and services in the city. The dominant force in triggering migration is the growth of the manufacturing sector. In a stagnating urban economy, no rural-urban migration will take place on any significant scale, as is seen in the case of Calcutta, where long years of stagnation have stopped rural-urban migration, and population growth is due entirely to natural increase.

In addition to being an employment multiplier, because additional job opportunities are created by the needs of the newly employed migrants, migration is a "demographic multiplier" because migrants are generally young, typically under thirty years old, and move to the cities during their most fertile years. Although the level of fertility in cities is lower than in the rural areas and migrants to the cities tend to have smaller families than those who stay behind, these facts are not enough to compensate for the migrants' age distribution, which is heavily concentrated in the child-bearing period. The effect of the demographic multiplier is longer lasting than that of the employment multiplier. Its magnitude is related to patterns of family formation and is rather country specific; it is related to the sex distribution of migration and depends on whether migration is predominantly an individual or a household move.

---

31. The close relation between the growth of urban activities and rural-urban migration in Korea is analyzed quantitatively in Bertrand Renaud, *Economic Fluctuations and Speed of Urbanization: A Case Study of Korea, 1955-1975,* World Bank Staff Working Paper no. 270 (Washington, D.C., November 1977).

Reducing Migration

One of the most remarkable and most disconcerting features of
policymakers in developing countries is their frequent unwilling-
ness to accept reasonable demographic projections in their planning for the capital region. They will insist on unrealistically low
figures with rather problematic consequences for the contents of
their decisions. As a result, public confidence in the validity of the
associated urban policies is greatly reduced when ten-year population projections are overtaken after two or three years. Very low
figures may be convenient to justify the suppression of investment
in the urban sector, but they delay the formulation of realistic
urban policies which would improve the internal efficiency of the
capital region. They also postpone the time when decentralization
policies will at last succeed in stemming migration into the area.

The effects of the demographic multiplier guarantee that the
population of the largest cities will continue to grow naturally by
large absolute numbers for quite a while. In addition, the largest
cities in each country, because of their sheer size, will absorb a
very high proportion of the total net migration flows into the
urban sector. Bringing the growth rate of the largest cities down
to their natural population growth rate—that is to say, bringing
net in-migration down to zero—will have a strong impact on other
cities and will require very serious planning. Smaller cities cannot
absorb the large number of migrants now moving to the capital
city without enduring growth rates three to four times higher than
at present. It is a matter of simple arithmetic to see that the
greater the concentration of population in the capital city, the
greater the flow of migrants to be redirected to smaller cities;
the number of migrants will be very large in relation to the current population of these cities.

This problem of redirecting migration to other cities is illustrated by the case of Colombian cities in 1951, 1964, and 1973
(see table 14). First, it can be seen that the attraction of large
cities can vary over time: during the first period, 42 percent of
the net migration flows converged on the largest cities; the proportion increased sharply to 78 percent during the second period,
accentuating population concentration further. Second, in both
periods migration was more important than natural growth as a

Table 14. *Migration and City Size in Colombia, 1951-73*
(population in thousands of persons)

City size (thousands)	Number of cities, 1973	1951 population	Population increase, 1951-64		1964 population
			Natural[a]	Migration	
1,500 and over	1	665	342 +	666	1,673
500-1,499	3	940	483 +	689	2,112
150-499	7	598	307 +	337	1,242
90-149	6	232	119 +	145	496
30-89	13	302	155 +	196	653
Small places	n.a.	1,732	890 +	295	2,917
Total urban population		4,469	2,296 +	2,328	9,093
Total Colombian population		11,548	5,936		17,484

n.a. Not available.

a. Natural population growth estimates are approximations based on the intercensal growth rates of the total population.

Source: Based on data from Johannes Linn, "Urbanization Trends, Polarization Reversal, and Spatial Policy in Colombia," paper presented to the Latin American Conference on Urban and Regional Policy, Bogotá, Colombia, July 1978, table 4.

source of population increase in Bogotá. Redirecting all net migration away from Bogotá during the second period to bring its growth back to the national rate of 2.69 percent would have sharply increased the growth of the smaller cities to rates above 6 percent. Similar exercises can be performed for any country, as can be easily inferred from the demographic materials presented in chapter 1.

In any given country, stabilizing the population of the capital city will remain a difficult task until the level of urbanization is sufficiently high (above 50 percent) and the population growth rate acceptably low (well under 1.5 percent). Until that stage is reached, the objective of national urbanization policies is to increase gradually the migration share of the smaller cities by improving their economic growth.

Redirecting migration away from the capital region implies the need for substantial changes in city-to-city as well as rural-urban migration flows. At higher levels of urbanization it is city-to-city migration that matters the most. Urbanized migrants are significantly more sensitive than rural-urban migrants to the

Population increase, 1964-73		1973 population	Intercensal growth rates	
Natural[a]	Migration		1951-64	1964-73
457 +	589	2,719	3.19 + 3.91	2.69 + 2.71
577 +	403	3,092	3.19 + 3.04	2.69 + 1.55
340 +	17	1,599	3.19 + 2.43	2.69 + 2.81
135 +	41	672	3.19 + 2.65	2.69 + 0.48
179 +	41	873	3.19 + 2.74	2.69 + 0.54
798 +	177	3,892	3.19 + 0.82	2.69 + 0.52
2,486	1,268	12,847	3.19 + 2.27	2.69 + 1.15
4,780		22,264	3.19	2.69

internal management of cities and the comparative merits of various places. This fact alone would justify better internal management of cities as an essential part of national urbanization policies in addition to the encouragement of industry outside the capital region.

Rural-Urban Interaction and Growth Linkages

There are strong two-way interactions between urban and rural development. Concerning urban-to-rural influences, a uniform finding in every country is that the most dynamic and productive agriculture is found near the most dynamic cities. Quite frequently, cities have developed originally because of the natural endowment of the area, but of more importance is that dynamic interactions continue to develop between the urban markets and farm producers. Because of their proximity to a large market, farmers can develop more intensive cash crops, they have easier access to suppliers, and they are in closer touch with government extension services as well as private farm suppliers, who constitute an important source of technical information. As the city market grows, more and more subsistence farmers are transformed partly or fully into commercial farmers. In addition, the city provides rural people in the area opportunities for part-time work. The dynamic growth of provincial cities tends to reduce the rural-urban economic gap that widens when economic growth is concentrated in distant large metropolitan centers.[32]

Conversely, a dynamic rural sector contributes to more rapid regional integration in all countries by raising farm incomes, purchasing power, and regional demand for both household goods and farm inputs. The development of rural-urban linkages assumes central importance for countries at low levels of urbanization where a substantial share of the national output comes from the farm sector, as in African countries south of the Sahara and in the large Asian countries. Indeed, in the South Asian countries the development of the rural sector should become by necessity a major element of a comprehensive national urbanization strategy.

Rural towns and small-scale cities are heavily dependent on the economic health of the farm sector, and their expansion is wholly dependent on the basic strategy for the expansion of agriculture. When a country becomes more industrialized, a rural growth strategy will not be the complete answer to problems of disparities in income levels between the rural sector and small towns on the one hand and the larger cities on the other. If studies have not shown the existence of diseconomies of scale for very large cities, they have shown the definite existence of diseconomies for smaller cities.

Because the level of capital intensity required in the production of consumer goods is low, it is widely expected that the demand structure associated with increasing rural incomes will be favorable to more decentralized and more labor-intensive patterns of industrialization. The results of studies in Malaysia qualify this view. On the one hand, the work done by Cohen, English, and Brookfield shows the high correlation between the three types of agriculture practiced in the region they studied and the pattern of growth of small towns.[33] On the other hand, the social accounting matrices (SAM) developed by the World Bank for the Muda

32. See Jin-Hwan Park, "The Growth of Taegu and Its Effect on Regional Agricultural Development," in *A City in Transition: Urbanization in Korea*, M. G. Lee and H. R. Barringer, eds. (Seoul: Hollym Corporation, 1971); and Bruce F. Johnston and Peter Kilby, *Agricultural Strategies, Rural-Urban Interactions and the Expansion of Income Opportunities* (Paris: Organisation for Economic Co-operation and Development [OECD], 1975).

33. Monique Cohen, John English, and Harold Brookfield, "Functional Diversity at the Base of the Urban System in Peninsular Malysia," *Journal of Tropical Geography* (forthcoming).

irrigation project clearly show that the demand leakages out of the region can be substantial, given the dichotomy between Malays and non-Malays in the settler population. Thus, in addition to the constraints placed by economies of scale, Malaysian regional development is affected by imperfect social integration.

In general, a strategy of rural development will have good effects on regional development and on the growth of regional cities. But it would be wrong to expect small economic leakages in the form of saving and demand for goods out of the region. The magnitude of the leakages depends on local economic organization and cannot be predicted without specific local surveys. Because of these economic leakages, rural development can yield increases in absolute income in the region but will not necessarily narrow the income gap with the rest of the economy, which benefits from the boost provided by the leakages.

Distribution of Rural Landholdings and Settlements Patterns

A skewed distribution of landownership will have a negative impact on the dynamics of settlements in both conspicuous and subtle ways. The rural sector in some countries is characterized by a bimodal distribution of landholdings: a few large landowners control the greatest proportion of the agricultural land, while a large number of small farmers have to make a living with the remainder. Such a situation is particularly conspicuous in Latin America, but not unique to that area. In 1960 in Peru, 3.3 percent of the landowners controlled 87.3 percent of the land; in Colombia, 9.1 percent controlled 85.8 percent.[34] Not incidentally, urban expansion in such countries is characterized by an increasing concentration of the urban population in the largest cities.

A highly skewed distribution of land creates three classes of people: the landless, who will easily migrate to cities for lack of rural ties; small landholders living at a subsistence level; and large-scale commercial farmers relying on hired labor. The stagnation of farm income affects urban development by leading to a low level of demand for both producer and consumer goods by the majority of

34. Food and Agriculture Organization [FAO], *Report on the 1960 World Census of Agriculture* (Rome, 1971). See also World Bank, *Land Reform* (Washington, D.C., May 1975), and T. James Goering, *Agricultural Land Settlement*, A World Bank Issues Paper (Washington, D.C., January 1978).

the population. Rural towns and small cities are based on small-scale, high-cost factor and product markets and serve a generally stagnant local economy. It becomes very difficult for any one of them to achieve a total income large enough to provide adequate economies of scale; because of very low household income levels, they would have to reach a much greater population size to reach an adequate economic scale. Depressed farm earnings and scarce employment opportunities in intermediate urban centers encourage migration to the large urban centers.

Unequal landownership can have many indirect effects which perpetuate the situation. For instance, in Argentina the generation of agricultural innovations by the public sector and the adoption of new technology by farmers are profoundly affected by the skewed distribution of landownership and the differences in the structure of production between small-scale farms and large-scale agricultural operations. It was found that small-scale farmers did not have domestic access to the yield-increasing technology that would be most effective in raising their incomes. The socioeconomic structure, together with market forces, yielded new technology consistent with the production methods of large-scale agricultural operations and not with those of small farmers. Conversely, rural development policies that provide an adequate technology to the large majority of small- and medium-scale farmers will, by raising their incomes, have a positive effect on national settlements patterns, particularly at low levels of development when agriculture is a dominant economic sector.

Intersectoral priorities can have a lasting effect on the structure of the urban sector and the distribution of population among cities of various sizes, and the size distribution of farms is an intervening factor. For instance, the Republic of Korea and Taiwan have many socioeconomic traits in common. In Korea, however, a much higher proportion of the urban population is concentrated in the capital city than in Taiwan. An important reason for this is that Korean agriculture is poorly endowed. In addition, the Korean growth strategy of the 1960s bypassed the agricultural sector to expand manufacturing. The combination of limited farm opportunities and the creation of manufacturing and other jobs in the Seoul region led to massive migration to Seoul. By the late 1960s the government was working to improve the terms of trade for the farm sector, in particular by establishing the

Grain Management Fund to support farm prices, an effort to limit the gap between rich industrial regions and poor agricultural regions. Because the land redistribution of 1949 had equalized landholdings in Korea, this policy improved the situation considerably. Now that the terms-of-trade and rural development policies are reaching diminishing returns, new policies are being devised to provide nonfarm employment opportunities in regional urban centers to minimize intersectoral and interregional disparities.[35]

Both the structure of the farm sector and the national policies concerning it are of great significance to the long-term evolution of national settlements. In countries marked by a highly skewed land distribution there are limits to what policies to improve farm terms of trade can do: small-scale farmers often operate at the margin of subsistence and cannot be reached easily through the market. Most of the benefits of favorable terms of trade will accrue to the large landowners and will leak back directly to the largest cities. Because of the limited market power of the small farmers, programs appropriate to their needs will be more difficult to initiate.

35. Because of the great uniformity of farm conditions, government extension policies for agricultural innovations have benefited a large percentage of farmers in Korea. The New Community Movement has also been extremely effective.

4

Current Status
of National Urbanization Policy

From an improved understanding of location decisions by business
firms and individuals and of the transmission of economic impulses from region to region, it is clear that the formulation of
national urbanization policy goes way beyond the problems of
concentration in the capital regions of middle-income countries.
It is time to return to the questions raised in the introduction and
to possible policy responses. What are appropriate objectives for
a national strategy that attempts to shift patterns of urban growth?
Can a national urbanization strategy operate apart from other
social and economic policies? Are there tradeoffs between a
greater dispersion of economic activities among various regions
and the rate of growth of the national economy? What actions
could or should be considered by a country to limit the growth of
the capital region? To what extent is it possible to channel economic activities through selected urban settlements? What policies
could be considered to improve rural-urban interactions?

Weakness of Policy in Developing Countries

Not a bad point of departure for a discussion of the urbanization strategies of developing countries is the evaluation recently
given by Brian J. L. Berry:

What characterizes most of the planning efforts in the Third
World is the absence of a will to plan effectively, and more
often than not, political smoke-screening. Most urbanization
policy is unconscious, partial, uncoordinated and negative. It
is unconscious in the sense that those who effect it are largely
unaware of its proportions and features. It is partial in that few

of the points at which governments might act to manage urbanization and affect its course and direction are in fact utilized. It is uncoordinated in that national planning tends to be economic and urban planning tends to be physical, and the disjunction often produces competing policies. It is negative in that the ideological perspective of the planners leads them to try to divert, retard or stop urban growth, and in particular to inhibit the expansion of metropolitan and primate cities.[1]

Fortunately for all concerned, things are not quite that simple or that bad in all countries. In his frustration Berry points to major problems that are very real. Of these four weaknesses, the lack of commitment and the lack of understanding are particularly damaging; competence in dealing with other problems can be improved over time through the process of learning by doing.

At present, many of the objectives selected by policymakers address the symptoms and not the causes of resource misallocation and severe regional disparities. The social and political objectives behind many announced spatial strategies are in clear conflict with the forces set in motion by national economic policy. The unintended spatial biases of national policy are yet to be more systematically considered, and more perceptive approaches are yet to be developed by national economic planners. It is, however, up to national physical planners to understand better the economic limitations of the explicit spatial strategies that they are advocating.

Better national urbanization strategies depend on improvements in the methods of planners. On the one hand are the national economic planners who are concerned only with the global or sectoral effects of their decision and ignore its spatial consequences. On the other hand are national physical planners, often in the ministries of public works or construction, who are heavily design oriented and, at times, appear more concerned with the maximization of their budget than with the overall economic impact of their grand designs. National economic planners must be made more aware that most of their decisions are not spatially neutral, and physical planners must acknowledge the limits placed

1. Brian J. L. Berry, "Comparative Urbanization Strategies," in *Managing Urban Systems*, Harry Swain and Ronald MacKinnon, eds. (Laxenburg, Austria: International Institute for Applied Systems Analysis, 1976), pp. 66-79.

on their plans by the state of the national economy, if national spatial policies are to improve the national environment.

Three Major Components

The proper formulation of a national urbanization strategy requires the systematic discussion of three major policy areas affecting patterns of population distribution and national settlements. The country must examine in turn: (1) the implicit spatial effects and biases of national policies; (2) the appropriate policies to deal with such problems of very large cities as congestion and pollution; and (3) the problems of regional inequality and the direct (explicit) policy instruments for the redistribution of economic activities. Of these three clusters of spatial policy instruments, the best known is the third, though the first two often have greater impact.

Every nation should take a different approach, geared to its social and political climate and its institutional structure. In chapter 2 the various factors that influence a country's ability to implement a national urbanization strategy were discussed, and it seems possible to rank the middle-income countries according to their likely ability to succeed. In discussing policy options, a variety of considerations makes it possible to avoid being somewhat taxonomic. It is necessary to consider the purpose and goals of the policies, the instruments used, the economic sectors affected, the spatial pattern that could be encouraged, the level of detail in decisionmaking at which the policy will operate, and so on.

Goals

The national urbanization strategy of a developing country always has multiple objectives, even though one or two may be emphasized in order to mobilize public opinion and to crystallize the order of priorities of decisionmakers in both the public and the private sectors. A multiplicity of objectives calls into use a comparable multiplicity of instruments, and the problem becomes one of identifying the combination of policies most appropriate for a given country at a given level of development. Another problem is to decide on the timing of policy decisions and the proper scheduling of spatial development programs.

Most planning efforts are initiated on the basis of the need for deconcentration of economic activities, when in fact the real problem lies with the intensity of dualism among various regions and locations in the countries. To organize a list of objectives of national urbanization strategies it is necessary to define more specifically the goals that could be selected to improve the situation:

1. *The integration of peripheral regions to increase the size of the national domestic market* (increasing the intensity of regional demand). Raising regional incomes to improve the demand for domestic products depends very much on rural development, agricultural policies, and the development of the transport and communications networks. This has often been the objective of large countries such as Brazil and Mexico, especially when they have adopted import-substitution industrialization strategies and consider it essential to increase domestic demand for new industrial products in order to reach greater economies of scale. Before defining spatial policies it would be useful to judge whether a country has already run the course of easy import substitution.

2. *The integration of peripheral regions and the opening up of new resources to raise the national output.* This objective applies to the mineral-rich countries such as Brazil, Mexico, and Iran, as well as the countries which still have an important resource frontier to exploit such as Malaysia or, again, Brazil. Water basin projects have often been developed under this heading, but they could just as well be classified under the first objective.

3. *The reduction of interregional disparities.* In a well-integrated society the concern for inequality among individuals or households should be more important than the concern for inequality between places. But the reduction of regional disparities is a legitimate concern in developing countries where regional differences are dramatic. In Latin America, for example, the output per capita of one region might be as much as ten times that of another, while in fully integrated, advanced economies the differences tend to be on the order of two to one.

4. *The more rapid development of border regions for reasons of national security.* This has been an important motivation for the Latin American region, where disputes have been frequent concerning the exact location of national boundaries in undeveloped regions. Similar incidents have occurred more recently between China and India; there, in anticipation of further inci-

dents, each country has developed a network of local roads
to consolidate its hold on disputed territory. A complete in-
ventory of international disputes of this type would place the
Middle East high on the list.

5. *Improvement of national political integration and social
cohesion within the nation.* It would be a conspicuous mistake
to assume that national urbanization strategies have purely economic objectives such as increasing output or redistributing
economic opportunities. In heterogeneous societies marked by
important cultural, political, and linguistic differences, a dominant
element of an urbanization strategy will be to maintain the cohesion of the state and to prevent regional minorities from, in some
fashion, leaving the national coalition of social groups. Special
institutions such as regional development corporations often give
visibility to the central government's concern for the region. They
are meant to be a vehicle for the transfer of resources and are one
expression of local political aspirations.

6. *Improvement of the national system of cities because of its
dominant role in the transmission of economic impulses and the
diffusion of innovations.* Raising the level of economic activity
in growing medium-size cities will help them reach sufficient economies of scale and will improve the interregional diffusion of
growth. It is often expected that a more developed system of
cities will help in equalizing access to the most important social
services such as education and public health.

Such strategic objectives are still much too broadly defined
to yield to analytical investigation. They must be further developed into specific programs and their related projects. For
instance, the formulation of a coherent and appropriate national
urbanization strategy will have a considerable impact on plans for
transport investment—the choice of network, the sectoral priorities (interurban as opposed to rural roads), as well as the timing of
investment. Additional elements which shape the national environment in major ways are water-basin development projects, the
location of large-scale industrial projects, or the structure of
networks for the distribution of electrical power. Similarly,
sectoral economic policies for agriculture, manufacturing, banking, and education will have significant unintended spatial effects.

Two important observations must be made with respect to the
multiple nature of the goals of a national urbanization strategy.

First, the selection of goals and the implementation of programs for a single region in isolation from the rest of the nation is a major reason for their ineffectiveness. Worthy objectives such as the maximization of per capita income over the planning horizon, the improvement of internal income distribution by reducing disparities between important minorities and the rest of the population, and the minimization of unemployment can often be found in conflict with national plans. In addition to possible conflict between the goals of maximizing both income and employment, plans for single regions may seriously underestimate the scarcity of human and capital resources at the national level to carry out the plan. Also, a regional strategy will often underestimate the mobility of resources between regions.[2]

Unintended Spatial Effects of National Economic Policy

For several important reasons, a good understanding of the unintended spatial effects of national economic policies (implicit spatial policies) is essential to developing countries. First, these policies have a definite effect on where people live and where they work, and they are present in all countries, including those that have no announced spatial policies. Second, in countries that have begun to tackle their spatial problems more seriously, the effect of the implicit incentives on business location decisions are much stronger than that of the official incentives. Third, if national economic policies can be adjusted so that their spatial biases in favor of the most advanced regions can be moderated, the need for specialized teams of spatial planners might be reduced and large-scale spatial planning postponed by a few years until more abundant planning skills are available. Furthermore, excessive population concentration in one region might be avoided altogether. The difficulty at present is that, though there is a good perception of the direction of most of these implicit effects, few effects, if any, have been measured quantitatively. No attempt has yet been made to compare the total monetary value of implicit incentives with the corresponding national budgetary resources

2. See, for instance, Benjamin Higgins's reevaluation of his previous experience with the separate regional plan for Pahang Tenggara in Malaysia, in *Regional Development and Planning*, Antoni R. Kuklinsky, ed. (Paris, London: Mouton, 1975).

devoted to explicit spatial policies. The accounting problems are indeed very serious.

The list of policy decisions and programs which are implemented without consideration of their spatial effects and which have potentially strong consequences for the distribution of population could be quite long. Moreover, a fine level of detail in evaluating the spatial effect of, say, a tariff would be necessary before making adjustments to neutralize that effect. It is enough here to list the main areas of concern. They can be taken in the order of their importance to national economic policy without prejudging the quantitative importance of each policy area to spatial development. They are: trade protection and industrial incentives by sector, foreign exchange policies, policy decisions affecting the rural sector, government regulation of economic activities (particularly of the energy sector), transport investment policies and regulations, the concentration of decisionmaking in the capital region, and the institutional structure. Policies concerning public enterprises may be considered an area of implicit spatial policy if a better spatial distribution of economic activity and employment is not one of their multiple objectives. Government procurement policies also can have a strong spatial impact.[3]

Trade Protection and Industrial Incentives

The protective effects of a foreign exchange policy will often discriminate against the sectors in the peripheral regions of a country because the national economic structure is differentiated between the capital (or core) region and the hinterland. Two quantitative studies of these effects have been done for Brazil.[4] They found significant regional disparities in the effects of eco-

3. In an extensive analysis done for the United States in 1970, a great deal of attention was given to procurement policies of the federal government. This factor is also increasingly important for some middle-income countries. It was found that, among forty-two spatial programs, only a few had a significant impact on the distribution of population; but activities such as defense and research and development had a strong impact. See U.S. Department of Commerce, Economic Development Agency, *Federal Activities Affecting the Location of Economic Development*, November 1970, 2 vols.

4. R. N. Barret, "The Brazilian Foreign Exchange Auction System: Regional and Sectoral Protective Effects," Ph.D. dissertation, University of Wisconsin, 1972; and O. E. Reboucas, "Interregional Effects of Economic Policies: Multi-Sector General Equilibrium Estimates for Brazil," Ph.D. dissertation, Harvard University, 1974.

nomic policies and that

> these regional disparities in the impact of protection are the
> result of differences in the structure of the regional economies.
> Protection tended most consistently to drive down the output
> of agriculture and non-tradeables and to stimulate the output of
> manufacturing industry. Since the latter generated a much
> smaller proportion of income in the North-East than the Center-
> South, even if the relative output changes in each sector had
> been the same in both regions, income would have risen more
> (or fallen less) in the latter.[5]

Further analytical work indicates that tariffs and industrial
incentives would have a differentiating effect on the location of
economic activities, even if no other forces were constraining the
location of industrial activities to a few favored locations, as is
actually the case.[6] A preliminary conclusion is that strong protection of industry will accentuate the concentration of population
and economic activities in a few locations and plant the seeds for
further cumulative imbalances. This analysis explains why countries which rely intensively on the growth of the manufacturing
industry and on international trade to develop their economy
while deemphasizing the agricultural sector are the most likely to
experience a strong surge of economic activity in a few major
urban regions.

What remains to be done is to estimate quantitatively the
spatial distributive effects of trade and industrial policies to have
a more accurate measure of their intensity. In a report on industrial incentives and effective protection in Nigeria, the Lagos
region, where much of the Nigerian industry is concentrated, is
shown to receive about 90 percent of the indirect subsidies provided by national trade policies. There is clearly an ongoing process of cumulative causation at work, leading to the greater concentration of activities in the Lagos area. Its correction will require a detailed and systematic look at the internal working of

5. Reboucas, "Interregional Effects," p. 6.

6. For a systematic theoretical assessment of the spatial effects of trade and in-
dustrial incentives, see Frances Ruane, "Trade and Industrial Incentives and the Spatial
Concentration of Economic Activities: Causal Relationships or Spurious Correlations?"
Urban and Regional Economics Division Working Paper no. 6 (Washington, D.C.: The
World Bank, Development Economics Department, 1979).

these policies and at how different locational patterns can be encouraged.

Sectoral Priorities and the Bias against Agriculture

In addition to the direct spatial biases of trade and industrial policies, an important problem lies in policies deliberately biased in favor of the industrial sector at the expense of the rural sector. This problem is becoming better understood, and the strength and limitations of import-substitution strategies are relatively well established. Their impact on urbanization patterns must be more systematically weighted in the formulation of national policies. The situation has been described earlier as follows:

> The implicit anti-agricultural bias in most import substitution policies has had a significant impact on urbanization patterns. Protection, by producing the distortions in prices in favor of manufacturing, stimulates these activities. This policy often leads to an import-dependent industrial structure. Because of protection, the real contribution of manufacturing activities, especially large-scale ones, has often been small. After correction for the effect of protection, there have been cases where the contribution of value added of a particular industry was actually negative. A dramatic example is that of Pakistan in 1963-64 where the average annual subsidy to large-scale manufacturing and the corresponding implicit tax on agriculture represented 6.6 percent of *total* domestic expenditures. The conventional contribution of industry was measured as 7.0 percent; its actual contribution after allowing for protection was estimated to be a dismal 0.4 percent of domestic value added. The implications for growth in the economy and consequent labor absorption from the next round of investment need hardly be labored. If the import substitution sector is producing little value added, the growth effect of the funds invested in it are effectively sterilized, and when apparent savings (i.e., part of the financial gains to owners of protected industry) are reinvested in similar industries, they merely perpetuate the cycle.[7]

7. See George Beier, Anthony Churchill, Michael Cohen, and Bertrand M. Renaud, *The Task Ahead for the Cities of Developing Countries*, World Bank Staff Working Paper no. 209 (Washington, D.C., 1975).

These kinds of policies toward the rural sector tend to generate problems of inefficiency in the large urban centers and depressed rural areas. A better treatment of the rural sector will have dynamic effects which will be much more supportive of the growth of the manufacturing sector and of the economy in general, as can be seen in the Ivory Coast in Africa.

Government Regulation of Economic Activities

Government regulation of economic activities also can have a profound impact on the economic dynamism of various regions and the distribution of population. The effects are felt, first, during the regulatory process when firms have to argue their case with government; second, they are felt once decisions have been reached and profitability is affected. In many developing countries the regulation of transport tariffs and the pricing of energy resources are frequently biased in favor of the capital region where residents pay less than the full cost of having goods and services delivered to them. The price of electricity in Mexico City is exactly the same as it is at the source some 1,000 kilometers away.[8] Reviewing the rationality and spatial effectiveness of tariffs and price regulations can only be done sector by sector for each country. For transport, freight tariff classifications and special commodity rates should generally reflect rather systematically the relative price per ton of various commodities (in addition to other considerations such as bulk, perishability, and scheduling of shipment). In general, finished goods pay much higher freight rates than intermediate goods or raw materials because production processes normally eliminate waste and add value. Locational problems arise when a discriminatory tariff is pushed to such a level that processing is always cheaper in the capital region, depriving other regions of opportunities for local growth and employment.

A minimum wage law can have a differentiated spatial impact which could be reinforced when coupled with a system of transfer payments to support the unemployed. Such a law provides incentives that stimulate the growth of the largest city. This is

8. In addition to improper pricing policies, the spatial impact of distribution networks is often in need of serious reconsideration. The issue lies more in the domain of explicit spatial policies and the provision of infrastructure.

because, in all countries, the effect of congestion costs on non-traded urban goods makes the cost of living in large cities higher than in small cities. Imposition of a minimum wage law which enforces a uniform wage rate for all cities will impose a higher real wage on industries located in small cities than on those located in large cities. If the demand for labor is elastic, there will be layoffs in the smaller cities, and workers will have an incentive to migrate to the large city, where the minimum wage rate is not yet effectively influencing industry. Migration risks will be reduced by unemployment welfare payments when such a program exists. The magnitude of the spatial bias can be appraised with adequate wage surveys and comparisons with the wages of workers not protected by the law.

Structure of Intergovernmental Fiscal Relations

In any country, large or small, the concentration of fiscal resources and decisionmaking stimulates the concentration of economic activities in the capital region. Fiscal centralization impedes the spatial distribution of economic activities for three major reasons. First, central decisionmakers insist on following stereotyped procedures in the name of efficiency and are sometimes ignorant of important local needs. Second, arguing with them is a costly process which leads to the progressive suppression of local initiative. Third, if central government officials have any bias, it is in favor of the capital region, which they know better and where they live. Central government officials commonly start with the premise that local officials are not very competent and should not be trusted, a self-fulfilling prophecy. The centralization of bureaucratic routines in the capital region also imposes severe costs in transaction time and money on individuals and businesses in other cities.

Finally, the structure of intergovernmental fiscal relations is important for the management of a national urbanization policy. In developing countries, local governments are often quite weak in their relations with the central government. One major reason is that the revenues of the central government are much more elastic than those of local government with respect to GNP increases because the central government has access to more buoyant tax bases. The urban development of the regions and population decentralization will be easier if local governments

share these taxes in a predictable manner.[9] Appropriate sources
of revenue for local governments allow them to provide services
more effectively for both the business sector and the resident
population. This improvement in services will release constraints
on business location.

Problems of Large Urban Concentrations

Many of the policies formulated toward the largest cities in
developing countries are regarded with great skepticism by local
residents and outsiders alike, because there is generally an obvious
mismatch between the problems associated with large concentrations of population in one urban area and the policies proposed
by the government to reduce the severity of these problems. Most
of these policies simply attempt to keep newcomers out of the
capital regions, without asking why people keep coming, and
generally ignore the fact that a significant proportion of growth
is due to the natural increase of the current city population. There
is often an inability to go to the source of the actual internal
problems—for lack of political will rather than for a lack of administrative skills—an inability which can be remedied over the
medium term in middle-income countries. A clarification of what
proper urban policies could do to improve the internal efficiency
of cities would greatly facilitate the formulation of national
settlements policies.

Primacy

An important distinction must be made between the concentration of a large percentage of the total urban population in the
largest city (primacy) and the existence of a very large urban center in a country. These two conditions are not necessarily found
in the same country. They should be distinguished on the basis of
what is known about economic efficiency and city size. Economic
efficiency for a city is the net result of the benefits of urban
agglomeration (agglomeration economies), which lowers the
average cost of production for many activities, and the losses
created by congestion and environmental deterioration. Most

9. See Woo-Sik Kee, "Fiscal Decentralization and Economic Development," *Public
Finance Quarterly*, vol. 5, no. 1 (1977).

studies show that, at the lower end of the size range, economies of scale increase rapidly as a city expands, but beyond a certain size the additional gains diminish rapidly. No study so far has been able to identify important diseconomies of scale (an upturn in the curve) with very large urban sizes.[10] This pattern has often been described as the "lazy-J" curve in studies of economies of scale.

At low levels of income and of urbanization, a country may have a high level of primacy, but the capital city may still barely have enough population and a high enough income level to provide an economically efficient environment. It would be poor policy to attempt to stop the growth of the only efficient city of the country. This does not mean that one should not look carefully for implicit economic policies which are subsidizing its growth at the expense of the rural sector. An examination of primacy level for 111 countries shows that primacy declines with per capita GNP and that there is a great deal of instability in the primacy index at low income levels (see figure 5).[11] At higher levels of income, the degree of primacy is less pronounced, and the real problem is the rapid growth of already very large cities (say, more than 2 million residents) when the average per capita income of the country is still low.

Economic Efficiency

In discussions of large cities, the main argument revolves around whether market failure is extemely intense and whether additional migration imposes a greater cost on the resident population than it contributes to increasing output so that there is a net loss to society. The existing empirical work deals mostly with U.S. cities, and its results are simply not transferable to the context of de-

10. Actual population figures for the economically efficient threshold should be used with caution because the average city income should be taken into account. A study done in India in 1968 identified a threshold size of 125,000, beyond which economies of scale were less pronounced. See *Cost of Urban Infrastructure for Industry as Related to City Size in Developing Countries: India Case Study*, a joint study of the Stanford Research Institute; School of Planning and Architecture, New Delhi; and Small Industry Extension Training Institute, Hyderabad, October 1968.

11. The estimated equation for the relation between primacy and the level of per capita GNP suggests that a 1 percent decrease in primacy is associated with a 3 percent increase in GNP per capita. This result is a strong one because primacy is estimated on the basis of metropolitan regions whenever applicable for the 109 cases.

Figure 5. Relation between Primacy and per Capita GNP

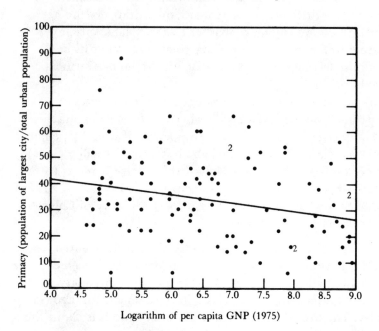

Logarithm of per capita GNP (1975)

Note: The number 2 refers to two identical observations. The sample contained 111 countries but only 106 are plotted; five outlyers are not on the chart.
Estimated equation: Primacy = 53.806 −2.9937 ln (GNP per capita).

veloping countries. The starting point is how urbanization affects national economic efficiency.[12] The three major questions asked are: What are the relations between city size and labor supply and demand? How do externalities affect city size? What would be the benefits of alternative city sizes? Negative externalities are due to the fact that transport congestion imposes a cost on workers who should be compensated in well-functioning labor markets. Similarly, a larger population concentration generates greater pollu-

12. For a nontechnical summary of the work done at the University of Chicago, see George Tolley and John Gardner, "Toward a Population Distribution Policy for America," in *Regional Economic Policy* (Minneapolis: Federal Reserve Bank, 1973). The full results of the Chicago Workshop are presented in George S. Tolley, Philip E. Graves, and John L. Gardner, *Urban Growth in a Market Economy* (New York: Academic Press, 1979). The most important theoretical work which extends significantly the earlier Chicago research is J. Vernon Henderson, *Economic Theory and the Cities* (New York: Academic Press, 1978).

tion. In determining whether a migrant should go to a smaller or a larger city, the difficulty is to estimate quantitatively the net social cost of adding one more worker to a very large city, by taking the difference between the marginal external costs he would impose in that city and those he would impose in an alternative location.

Empirical analysis requires consideration of economies of scale in production, the effect of local public finance externalities (in larger cities there is a larger proportion of wealthy people, and tax rates relative to income will be less than in smaller cities), and the effect of minimum wage laws (which drive workers to larger cities and also raise unemployment costs). In the case of the United States, the research done at the University of Chicago has been summarized as follows:

> The effects of the externalities on city size are substantial, while the national income costs of the city size effects are extremely small. The basic reason for the substantial city population effect is the high elasticity of demand for labor in the city. The production function for many goods is about the same all over the country, so that a small change in wage costs will induce larger changes in industry location decisions. The basic reason for the smallness of national income costs of migration to the largest cities is that, for laborers reallocated, the difference in their marginal products as between locations is a relatively small percentage of their total marginal product. The specific numbers used and details of the analytical assumptions could vary a great deal and still not alter the basic message.[13]

In other words, the central finding of the Chicago Workshop is that, in the United States, the failure to make new migrants pay for the costs of traffic congestion and environmental damage that they impose on present residents does not imply a large loss of efficiency for the national economy; this failure does, however, make a difference for the city which experiences a substantial population gain. The main value of this finding for large developing cities is to show that policies dealing with the internal operations of large cities are important to national settlements

13. Tolley and Gardner, "Toward a Population Distribution Policy for America."

patterns. The results of other U.S. studies either failed to identify an upper limit to the efficiency of large cities or found a discontinuity in the range of efficient city sizes, with some intermediate-size cities failing to meet the test.[14]

No one should be particularly surprised at the difficulty of reaching decisive results on the relation between city size and economic efficiency as broadly defined in these studies. The difficulty increases further when other important factors are included in the analysis, as they should be: the size of a city is not unrelated to the composition of its output; a given city must be considered as part of the total system of cities; and the proximity of another large city affects its growth potential. In addition, the problems of market failure affecting the location decisions of business firms are of a much greater magnitude in developing countries. The most thorough, but purely theoretical, analysis of the problems of an efficient allocation of resources in a system of cities concludes:

> In general there is a problem of population allocation among cities. Given an economy with multiple types of cities and a few cities of each type, if there are external economies of scale in production or pure public goods in consumption, federal government intervention will be needed to ensure an efficient allocation of resources among regions.[15]

This new theoretical effort, which has not yet been put to an empirical test, at least encourages the view that there is a problem with the largest size. It remains a different matter to make a dogmatic claim that 3 million or 6 million or even 10 million people within a metropolitan region are too many.[16]

An important reason for distinguishing between the problems of city size in developing countries and advanced economies is the fact that middle-income countries in particular are living

14. David Segal, "Are There Returns to Scale in City Size?" *Review of Economics and Statistics*, vol. 53 (1976), pp. 339-50; and Aaron Yeser and Sidney Goldfarb, "An Indirect Test of Efficient City Size," *Journal of Urban Economics*, vol. 5 (1978).

15. J. Vernon Henderson, *Economic Theory and the Cities* (New York: Academic Press, 1978), chap. 4, p. 98.

16. Henderson clearly addresses the issue of large, multicentered metropolitan regions. For him a suburban center becomes a distinct urban area when it becomes a major employer, drawing commuters from the area adjacent to it and all points beyond it (away from the central business district).

through the most rapid phase of their urbanization. There is a sharp contrast between the expanding urbanization of developing economies and the mature urbanization of advanced economies, as detailed earlier. Among the many contrasting characteristics of expanding and mature urbanization the major difference is that rural-urban migration has run its course and urban-urban migration is the main factor affecting the distribution of urban growth in advanced economies. Given a numerically rather static labor force, the relative efficiency of various city sizes may become directly apparent through the revealed preferences of urban residents.

A recent international comparison of eighteen countries indicates that mature urbanization renders the largest cities less attractive to economic activities and supports the labor market analysis by Tolley and Gardner (high elasticity of demand for labor in large cities). Vining and Kontuly have found that, of the eighteen countries they studied, eleven were

> showing either a reversal in the direction of net population flow from their sparsely populated, peripheral regions to their densely populated core regions or a drastic reduction in the level of this net flow. In seven of them this reversal or reduction became evident only in the 1970's. Six countries have yet to show an alteration in the movement of persons into their most densely populated regions. Some possibly unreliable British data likewise fail to reveal a slackening in the "drift South" of the British population.[17]

The Vining-Kontuly study deals not with the largest urban areas as such but with more broadly defined core regions and underlines the changing characteristics of urban systems when they are driven by urban-urban mobility patterns. Another remarkable finding is that the decline of the core region is prevented by foreign immigrants, particularly in France, Sweden, and Norway.

As noted earlier, there are few developing countries in which the rural population has even begun to decline, and in all of them,

17. See Daniel R. Vining and Thomas Kontuly, "Population Dispersal from Major Metropolitan Regions: An International Comparison," *International Regional Science Review*, vol. 3, no. 1 (1979), pp. 49-73. The first seven countries where dispersal began in the 1960s were Japan, Sweden, Norway, Italy, Denmark, New Zealand, and Belgium. The next four countries are France, the Federal Republic of Germany, the German Democratic Republic, and the Netherlands. The six countries where a slowdown has not yet started are Hungary, Spain, Finland, Poland, the Republic of Korea, and Taiwan.

rural-urban migration continues to expand the population of all cities. Given the structure of the labor market and the constraints on business location, the likelihood of a reversal in population concentration in the immediate future is not very great. Policies designed to improve the internal efficiency of the largest cities must therefore be vigorously pursued and not side-stepped in the name of decentralization. The Tokyo metropolitan region was the first city to enter a range of population sizes surpassing that of Western countries. It is already clear that some metropolitan regions of the middle-income countries will be going even further, such as Mexico City and São Paulo. It will take some time before the correction of implicit biases in national policies and the implementation of more effective spatial policies begin to make a difference at the margin, given the large reservoir of low-income, rural-urban migrants in Mexico and Brazil.

New Towns and New Capitals in Developing Countries

Influenced by Western countries, many middle-income countries have been attempting to develop growth-center strategies and have considered programs of "new towns." These are two very distinct elements of urbanization policy which should be treated separately. New towns are often associated by urban theorists with the idea of optimal city size. In the realm of actual policymaking, planning for new towns should be strongly discouraged in most developing countries.

"New towns" refer to entirely new, planned urban communities clearly detached from the commuting zone of existing cities. They are expected to provide employment to their resident population and to attract business firms and industries which will form the economic base of the city. New-town programs should be clearly distinguished from the development of large-scale neighborhoods at the fringe of larger urban areas. The new suburbs of Singapore or the Republic of Korea are frequently called new towns to emphasize a sense of progress and modernity and also because they require large-scale planning. They can be quite large and have more than 12,000 housing units. But these new neighborhoods are well within commuting distance to the major sources of jobs in an existing city. The design standards of these new communities vary according to location and can be geared to prevalent income levels in the city. Public facilities are immedi-

ately available, and there is no investment threshold to cross in
providing services since internal neighborhood networks of roads
and utilities are connected to the existing city system. The population of the new neighborhood can relocate in other parts of the
city as circumstances permit, and new residents will easily replace
them.

New towns are, however, a poor way to seek a better balance
among various cities and to alleviate congestion in old urban centers. They have problems, whether they are intended to be industrial, residential, or new capital cities. Although urban de-
signers and architects are fascinated by the concept of new towns,
they frequently have a fundamental misunderstanding of urbanization and play on the desires of the upper-income groups to cut
themselves off from urban pollution and congestion by creating
fully planned, well-designed "garden cities." The construction of
new towns raises questions of urbanization rationale, costs,
methods of financing, economies of scale, localization, and manpower and planning capabilities. They present problems in properly identifying the sources of growth of an urban community: too
often, new towns are planned for a single purpose and are dependent for long periods (more than ten years) on faltering
political support. They also present important problems of internal spatial organization and design.

One reason for avoiding new towns in developing countries is
that new towns have never lived up to the claim that they were a
particularly good way of absorbing urban population. Even on the
largest scale, they will never absorb more than a very small percentage of the total annual increment of the national urban
population. Brasilia, which is one of the most dramatic examples
of a new city, had a population in 1970 (after more than ten
years of investment and settlement) that was about the same size
as the annual increment of the population of São Paulo.

A second critical reason for avoiding new towns in middle-
income countries is that they constitute the most expensive way
of financing urban development. The universal experience with
new towns is that they are capital-intensive experiments, and the
cost of living there tends to be significantly higher than in existing
cities. An additional undeniable feature in developing countries is
that a separate town grows in the shadow of the planned, highly
serviced new town. Living in the well-designed new town are those

for whom it has been designed—mostly high-income groups financially capable of living in the city. Outside the planned jurisdiction of the new town is a shadow town, unplanned, poorly serviced, with a very low-income population. Here live the construction workers and other unskilled laborers who were attracted to the area during the construction period and remained after the boom, commuting to the official new town for some sort of employment. This has occurred in the cases of Brasilia, Islamabad, Chandighar, and other lesser cities (see Appendix C).

Because new towns in developing countries are dependent on subsidies (open or hidden), their situation is not consistent with the generally pronounced scarcity of resources in the rest of the country. At a time when many existing cities lack adequate water supply, drainage, sewerage, public transport, and low-income housing, new towns compete with old cities for central government funds. High standards, high costs, low economic returns, and high maintenance costs make new towns inaccessible to most of the population and are inconsistent with prevailing levels of urban income.

In a sound urban development environment, public land development costs can be financed through municipal taxes, public utility costs can be financed through user charges, and housing and residential land development can be financed through rental fees. The problem is that the capital and operating costs of new towns rise rapidly to levels that require a typical household to spend more than 50 percent of its income (often after substantial subsidies) on housing and utilities. In the provision of housing, for instance, there is a strong inducement to shift design standards upward to serve the needs of the very rich, who are the only ones capable of paying cash. If a normal cross-section of urban households is to afford them, the cost of utilities and housing should be commensurate with their income levels.

New capital cities represent a very special kind of new town. They are the outcome of a fundamentally political decision and cannot be directly compared with other new towns. Among their many objectives, they are expected to be a symbol for the entire nation (Ankara, Islamabad, Canberra, Brasilia) and a model for the modernization of many existing cities and future new cities. But their planners must still search for an adequate economic structure to diversify the employment base. Long-term problems

arise for the city when insufficient attention is given to the socioeconomic structure and future growth. The planned socioeconomic composition of the population and its employment base are
substantially more important for the eventual success of the
capital then the issue of city design and physical layout. Rarely,
if ever, do planners ask themselves whether the resources com-
mandeered by the new capital could be more efficiently used for
other urban purposes and serve a greater proportion of the national populaṭṭn than the civil servants who will live there. There
has yet to be a planning document for a new capital city that
investigates the costs and benefits for the option of not building
it.

Regional Inequalities, Dualism, and Spatial Policy

In practically all countries, spatial policies have as objectives
the economic, political, and social integration of all regions in
accordance with national values. Integration is indeed the ultimate
objective if it is taken to mean the easy mobility of resources and
people between regions and economic sectors as well. This objective is constantly in evolution and is translated into programs
such as the development of depressed or undeveloped areas (the
western region of the Republic of Korea), new settlements for
agricultural development (Malaysia, Latin America, and Indonesia), new settlements near newly discovered mineral resources
(the east coast of Mexico), the restructuring of major metropolitan regions (São Paulo and Seoul), the strengthening of other
developed regions, intensified policies of river basin development
(Mexico), or the development of border areas for economic and
strategic reasons (Mexico, Brazil, and Paraguay). It could even
include the devolution of power and decentralization of decisionmaking, even though this is one of the most difficult steps to carry
out in any country.

The spatial policies developed in advanced economies differ
significantly from those of most middle-income countries, since
advanced economies have been strongly stimulated by the concern
for greater equality. In developing countries there are much
greater opportunities for convergence between the desire to reduce
disparities among regions and the need to improve the overall
efficiency of the national economy. In many middle-income

countries there are pronounced differences between regions. Dualism exists not as a gradation of different levels of technology and scale; it is discontinuous, with the differences between regions extemely pronounced and resource mobility very restricted.

The great economic and social differences between regions sharply distinguishes the problems of a large number of developing countries from those of advanced economies. Even when blunt, macroeconomic indicators are used, such as estimates of the gross regional product (GRP), the contrast is very clear.[18] In most advanced economies, the ratio between the poorest and the richest region is on the order of two to one; in many middle-income countries this ratio can go up to ten to one, as can be seen in table 15 where data for seventeen countries are reported. To account for the differences in the size of the population of each region, the population-weighted index originally proposed by Jeffrey Williamson is also presented.[19] By that index, tco, most middle-income countries, particularly in Latin America, have indicators of inequality twice as large as those of advanced economies. This contrast between the richer, more advanced regions and the poorer regions has led to differentiating the core region of a country from its periphery and to the notion of "polarized development."[20]

There is little doubt that these pronounced spatial inequalities are associated with the biases of national economic policies discussed earlier. The problems of generating growth with equity are also strongly felt in the formulation of national urbanization policies. Little is known about the dynamics of regional inequalities in the case of developing countries; different countries are

18. GRP estimates are only blunt indicators of regional disparities for at least two important reasons. First, they do not provide a precise picture of economic conditions in each region; more specific and more microeconomic performance indicators are needed for planning. Second, there are serious problems of quality, and comparisons between countries or over time are only approximate.

19. Jeffrey G. Williamson, "Regional Inequality and the Process of National Development: A Description of the Patterns," *Economic Development and Cultural Change*, vol. 13 (July 1965), pt. 2.

20. John Friedmann has attempted to articulate this notion of polarized development as it cuts across all important aspects of human activities in an intuitively very stimulating, but quantitatively untested (untestable?), "theory of polarized development" in *Urbanization, Planning and National Development* (Beverly Hills: Sage, 1973). In policymaking, however, it is hard to hold dogmatically the view that only the quantifiable is important.

Table 15. *Regional Disparities Based on Gross Regional Product*

Country	National per capita GRP (1976 U.S. dollars)			Williamson factor[a]	GRP per capita (1976 U.S. dollars)		
	1976	Estimate	Year of estimate		Richest region	Poorest region	Richest/Poorest
Netherlands	6,200	3,375	1970	0.1403	4,032	2,578	1.56
Belgium	6,780	3,645	1970	0.1604	4,380	2,616	1.67
Italy	3,050	2,488	1970	0.2718	3,384	1,538	2.20
Germany, Fed. Rep. of	7,380	4,371	1970	0.1352	7,022	2,683	2.62
Japan	4,910	3,274	1972	0.3007	5,555	1,900	2.92
France	6,550	3,989	1970	0.2430	5,918	2,833	2.09
United Kingdom	4,020	3,197	1970	0.1088	3,667	2,566	1.43
India	150	149	1964-65	0.1845	217	97	2.24
Korea, Rep. of	670	373	1970	0.3078	582	270	2.16
Thailand	380	502	1975	0.6775	1,358	215	6.34
Iran[b]	1,936	774	1972	0.9226	3,132	313	10.07
Colombia	630	838	1975	0.3073	1,342	199	6.75
Mexico	1,090	521	1970	0.5343	1,067	198	5.39
Brazil	1,140	440	1969	1.6201	1,102	109	10.14
Venezuela[b]	2,570	1,729	1971	0.5333	3,175	502	6.32
Malaysia	860	438	1970	0.3599	730	202	3.62
Yugoslavia	1,680	740	1968	0.3570	1,354	237	5.72
Argentina[b]	1,550	1,561	1970	0.3132	3,706	397	9.33

Note: The GRP per capita figures refer to the year for which the disparities are estimated. To facilitate comparisons with more recent conditions in 1976, all figures have been translated into 1976 U.S. dollars.

a. An index consisting of a coefficient of variation adjusted for the relative population of each region. Jeffrey G. Williamson, "Regional Inequality and the Process of National Development: A Description of the Patterns," *Economic Development and Cultural Change*, vol 13 (July 1965), pt 2.

b. Includes oil.

Source: Various national documents and World Bank files.

seen to have different experiences, but there are no reliable methodologies to explain their divergent paths.

Not much comparative work has been done on regional inequalities beyond that of Williamson and his cross-country comparisons, which were based on a sample with a large proportion of Western countries.[21] And since the quality of statistical information is highly correlated with the wealth of a country, the degree of comparability among countries is an open question. From a cross-section of twenty-four countries, Williamson concluded that interregional inequality appears greater at intermediate levels than at low or high levels of development. He advanced the idea of an inverted U curve between interregional inequality and development and raised in the spatial context the question whether regional inequalities are an inevitable part of development. But inequalities of the magnitude observed in certain Latin American countries or in the Middle East are not merely an undesirable side effect of growth; they are a major problem.

Tradeoff between Regional Income Equality and National Growth

Some of the most systematic work on the tradeoff between interregional income equalization and economic efficiency has been done in Japan. It was initiated by the Economic Planning Agency, which wanted to determine how national growth might suffer from the use of regional policy instruments in such areas as transport, infrastructure investment, and industrial decentralization.[22] The model was based on a relatively short sample period (1955-62) and on nine regions regrouping forty-six prefectures. It yielded a significant tradeoff between the national growth rate and more regional income equality. It projected that, if national income increased by 175 percent in eight years, the coefficient of variation of the regional per capita incomes would increase at 3 percent a year. It also projected that, if industrial investment were

21. See also Alan G. Gilbert and David E. Goodman, "Regional Income Disparities and Economic Development: A Critique," in *Development Planning and Spatial Structure*, Alan G. Goodman, ed. (New York and London: John Wiley, 1976), pp. 113-42.

22. Japan Economic Planning Agency, *A Study on Japan's Nationwide Regional Econometric Model* (Tokyo: Economic Research Institute, 1967). This study is in Japanese, but other related papers have been published in English by the Japan section of the Regional Science Association. The most significant empirical study in the field is Koichi Mera, *Income Distribution and Regional Development* (Tokyo: University of Tokyo Press, 1975), in English.

decentralized, the coefficient of variation would decline, but at a significant loss to the national growth rate. Improvements in transport between developed and less developed regions would lead to greater growth with a rather neutral effect on regional disparities.

As usual, the familiar warning applies that "it does require maturity to realize that models are to be used but not to be believed."[23] These Japanese studies have uncovered some important relationships for regional policies, but these findings are at the margin for Japan over a short period and in the absence of major structural change. Without similar studies in distinctly different countries, such as Latin America, it is not possible to draw strong inferences from this Japanese work; it merely indicates more precisely where to look for interesting regional policy instruments.

Using the same data base, Koichi Mera explored the relation between productive efficiency in different regions of Japan and the spatial density of economic activities (urbanization). Because the Japanese data are extremely detailed and include estimates of the stock of social overhead capital, it was possible to estimate regional production functions based on three factors of production: labor, private capital, and social overhead capital, which were later disaggregated further.[24] From the estimated production functions, Mera derived estimates of the marginal productivity of various forms of capital investment for the national economy:

> On this basis the following tentative conclusions can be derived: the production elasticity of social capital in the primary sector is 22 percent, that in the secondary sector about 20 percent without social capital in transportation and communication and more than 50 percent with it, and that in the tertiary sector in the range of 12 to 18 percent. The above estimates are tentative in the sense that they are sensitive to the specification of the estimating equation.[25]

23. Henri Theil, *Principals of Econometrics* (New York: John Wiley, 1971), preface.

24. See Mera, *Income Distribution*; or "Regional Production Functions and Social Overhead Capital: An Analysis of the Japanese Case," *Regional and Urban Economics*, vol. 3 (May 1973). Data on the social capital stock included estimates of primary sector capital (such as soil and water conservation, flood control, and irrigation), coastal improvements, industrial water supply, vocational training, power and gas, transport and communication, and health, education, and welfare facilities, including public housing.

25. Mera, *Income Distribution*, p. 130.

These findings for Japan represent the first systematic attempt to look at the effect of the composition of public investment programs on the productivity of the national economy. In particular, the high productivity of transport and communication investment is indicative of the bottlenecks in the Japanese economy at the time: the number of private cars was then increasing at rates of between 20 and 30 percent a year.

The tradeoff between more national growth and greater regional equality may have been overemphasized by the studies based on the Japanese data for the thirteen-year period from 1954 to 1967. In the countries of East Asia which are fairly well integrated economically, it appears that deliberate policies, particularly those dealing with the rural sector and farm income, can be effective in moderating or reducing regional disparities. In figure 6 the range of GRP per capita (the difference between the richest and the poorest province, measured in relation to the national average) and the dispersion of GRP per capita (measured by the coefficient of variation) are plotted against the national per capita income (based on 1963 = 100) for the Republic of Korea. In spite of the tremendously rapid growth of the economy, when per capita GNP increased 2.4 times, regional disparities, after a sudden increase, fell markedly and steadily to a new low. This trend is also confirmed by the coefficient of dispersion. A similar trend can be found in the case of Japan.[26] Such results do not give strong support to the dilemma between growth and regional equity anticipated by the Japanese Economic Planning Agency. At present both the Korean and the Japanese governments find it vexing that regional disparities still remain, but the nature of their problem is quite different from that of most developing countries, which face large disparities because of the lack of market integration. Instead, the problems of regional and interpersonal inequality in Korea and Japan are more often due to the fact that some social groups are not easily reached through the market and are not economically or geographically very mobile. These are welfare problems as commonly understood in developed countries.

When there is a great lack of integration among regions of the same country, the cost of living will vary markedly among them.

26. For a comparison of Japan and Korea, see Koichi Mera, "Population Concentration and Regional Income Disparities: A Comparative Analysis of Japan and Korea," in *Human Settlement Systems*, Niles M. Hansen, ed. (Cambridge, Mass.: Ballinger, 1978).

Figure 6. National Growth and Regional Income Disparities in the Republic of Korea, 1962-74

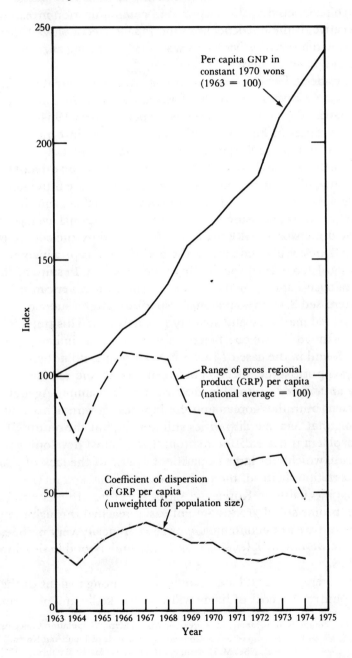

Per capita GNP in constant 1970 wons (1963 = 100)

Range of gross regional product (GRP) per capita (national average = 100)

Coefficient of dispersion of GRP per capita (unweighted for population size)

Index

Year

122

This is particularly clear in a recent analysis of levels of poverty
in various parts of Peru.[27] The cost of living in the region of
Lima was found to be about 60 percent higher than in the poorest
region (La Selva). In such a case regional differences based on un-
adjusted per capita income figures will overemphasize the income
gaps between regions. Under these circumstances the advanced
countries' dilemma of what to do with their depressed regions and
the running debate on "place prosperity" versus "people prosperity" take on an intensely different color.

In developing countries the best ground for national concern
with interregional inequalities derives from their significance as
indicators of poor integration and the misallocation of resources.
Some cases may call for reallocating resources to more dynamic
regions where labor productivity and earnings may be higher or
which may offer a better location for industry. In other cases
analysis may show that the need is not so much for a reallocation
of labor and industry as for complementary investment in human
capital, through more education or more investment in social and
economic infrastructure which cannot be provided profitably by
the private sector. In many cases regional inequalities may be
moderated by reorganizing the structure of inputs and product
markets or by eliminating institutional arrangements that discourage investment in the lower-income region.

Large regional disparities are a sign of a serious problem of
socioeconomic integration, but past a certain level (say, when the
range of GRP per capita falls somewhat below three to one) more
precise and more detailed microeconomic indicators are necessary.
The reason is that perfect socioeconomic integration will not
enrich a region with a poor comparative advantage: satisfactory
integration does not imply a high rate of expansion in every
peripheral area. For instance, the historical record shows that
in the United States regional disparities have never been as extreme as those observed in many developing countries, because the
degree of socioeconomic mobility has generally been satisfactory.
Regional disparities have not vanished completely, however. The
range of per capita personal income (not GRP) over 110 years,

27. See Vinod Thomas, "The Measurement of Spatial Differences in Poverty: The
Case of Peru," World Bank Staff Working Paper no. 273 (Washington, D.C., January
1978).

standardized over the national average (U.S. = 100), was:[28]

	1860	1880	1900	1920	1940	1960	1970
Highest	143	141	139	136	132	117	114
Lowest	65	43	45	53	49	66	74
Ratio	2.20	3.28	3.09	2.57	2.69	1.77	1.54

Regional and Interpersonal Inequalities

Explicit regional policies should be supported by systematic efforts to correct the implicit biases of national economic policies, including their distributive effects. Too often, regional policies are used by policymakers as the politically cheapest way to appear to confront problems of interpersonal inequalities. If income redistribution is really the objective, explicit regional policies can be helpful, but they come a very poor second behind other forms of income redistribution (such as land reforms, reform of the fiscal system, pricing policies, or education policies). Moreover, the exact content of regional programs and projects must be carefully examined, because in many countries the poorest regions are also those with the most skewed income distribution. It would be very unfortunate if the benefits of regional policies accrued mostly to the highest income groups. It is necessary to evaluate the local income benefits of all sector programs, particularly those directly addressed to the private sector. For instance, income-raising methods other than the tax relief under the 34/18 program for Brazil's Northeast might have been more efficient and more equitable.[29]

Regional Investment, Local Multiplier Effects,
and Leakages through the Urban System

The assumption that rapid investment in a region will have strong trickle-down effects locally is indeed just an assumption. It must be carefully checked against local and national conditions. There are no simple guidelines as to the size of the regional multiplier and the extent of leakage to be expected from a given project. A well-designed project will contribute to raising local

28. See Richard A. Easterlin, "Regional Income Trends, 1840-1950," in *American Economic History*, Seymour E. Harris, ed. (New York: John Wiley, 1961); and U.S. Department of Commerce, *Statistical Abstract of the United States*, 1978.
29. See David Goodman, "Industrial Development in the Brazilian Northeast: An Interim Assessment of the Tax Credit Scheme of Article 34/18," in *Brazil in the Sixties*, R. J. A. Roett, ed. (Nashville: Vanderbilt University Press, 1972).

income but may not reduce interregional income differentials much because many of the financial flows will leak back to the large urban centers through the urban network. This can be illustrated by the case of an agricultural project in Malaysia and the industrial dispersion policy of Japan.

An Agricultural Example: The Muda Region Project in Malaysia. The Muda River Valley project in Malaysia is a well-studied example of a large, highly visible public sector project, located in a backward region as a major element of a regional policy designed by the central government. The Muda irrigation project covers a command area of about 100,000 hectares cultivated by about 51,000 farm families. Most of the region is devoted to the monoculture of rice. The introduction of irrigation permitted double-cropping, and the scheme brought a substantial rise in the total output of paddy as well as in local farm incomes. At present, the Muda region, which represents only 6 percent of Malaysia's population, meets about 40 percent of Malaysia's annual rice requirements. In 1965, before the project, the region had a per capita GDP of about 60 percent of the national average; the problem is that, after successful completion of the project, it is still at about the same relative level. Thus, "although the Muda Scheme had done much to raise incomes by 1972, it had not solved the region's poverty problem."[30]

The construction of a social accounting matrix for the scheme has clarified this puzzling situation. The social structure was divided into five groups: (1) landless paddy workers, (2) labor-abundant paddy farms, (3) land-abundant paddy farms, (4) other agricultural households, and (5) nonfarm households. It was found that almost all landless paddy workers and a great proportion of labor-abundant paddy farms, or about 15 percent of the population, still fell below the Malaysian-defined poverty line.

The social accounting matrix was used to show that the inter-industry linkages within the region were very limited. The downstream effects of the projects were mostly felt through final demand. The leakages were substantial, and household final

30. See Clive Bell, "Some Aspects of Regional and Cost-Benefit Analysis within a Social Accounts Framework: With Special Reference to the Muda Region of Malaysia," paper presented at the Conference on Social Accounting Methods in Development Planning, Cambridge, England, 1978, p. 19.

expenditures accounted for just over 50 percent of total imports. For these imports, which were mostly durables, the ratio of noncompetitive to competitive imports for household consumption exceeded seven to one. Clearly, the local urban centers could not provide the appropriate goods. Only 45 percent of regional private savings found its way into regional investment. More strikingly, "the annual outflow of regional private savings in 1972 was almost 20 percent of the total investment in the Muda Scheme by the Malaysian Government and the World Bank."[31] The capital outflow attributable to households and regionally based firms was almost 10.5 percent of regional value added. Estimates of government flows show a net tax burden for the region even though the area is poorer than average.

How did that happen? In addition to the apparently inappropriate federal fiscal policies, it appears that about half the total increase in household incomes accrued to nonfarm households. The scope for private on-farm investment was limited for farm households, and the problem may have been compounded by the fact that non-Malays are not permitted to own farm land and have concentrated in trade and services, transferring their net savings outside the region for higher rates of return. The Muda case shows how important it is to determine the extent to which different classes of households (and different types of firms) have different propensities to invest in the region itself because of imperfections in the capital markets and different barriers to entry for different social categories according to economic activities.

An Industrial Example: Japan in 1960. Japan, which has traditionally had a low degree of income inequality on a national basis, has grown extremely rapidly since World War II, placing much emphasis on the growth of the manufacturing sector. By the middle of the 1960s the Japanese felt that the rapid growth of the 1955-61 period had led to serious imbalances in the rates of growth of various prefectures.

The Japanese defined their regional problem by regional income differentials, widening productivity differentials, the excessive concentration of population in big cities, a distorted accumulation of productive capacity in particular districts, and a shortage

31. Ibid., p. 25.

of industrial water in important coastal areas, as a result of which the underground water table had fallen and caused the ground to sink, as in Tokyo Bay. The rapid rate of industrialization had spread smog in big cities, aggravated traffic conditions, and contributed to a rapid rise in consumer prices.[32]

A first investigation led to the conclusion that, in contrast to interindustry and intraindustry scale differentials, the regional differentials in per capita income and productivity are relatively unlikely to disappear. Although it was popularly agreed that regional differentials in per capita income and productivity had widened during the process of rapid growth, this could not be substantiated statistically. When the prefectures were divided into two subgroups, the industrialized and the nonindustrialized, it was found that the regional differentials had widened between the two groups, but *within* each group, differentials had been significantly reduced. The two conflicting tendencies led to a fairly stable situation overall. When the manufacturing sector was further subdivided into heavy industries and light industries, it was found again that within-group differentials tended to decrease over time and that the major source of possible increases in the regional income differential would be the rate of growth of heavy industry. In studying regional variations in value added per worker, it was predictably found that heavy industry and a concentration of large firms contribute to higher levels of regional differentials.

Of particular significance in discussing the potential of industrial dispersion for equalizing regional income was the contrast between the level of value added per capita in various regions and the corresponding level of per capita income. There is a significant difference between productivity and per capita income rankings. The ratio of income to gross value added in new heavy-industry prefectures was particularly low. Some of the gross value added created inside a prefecture flows to the head office of corporations or other industries outside the prefecture. Investment in large capital-intensive projects will spawn complementary industries consisting of parts makers, specialized suppliers, and the like,

32. See Miyoei Shinohara, *Structural Changes in Japan's Economic Development,* Economic Research Studies no. 11 (Tokyo: Hitotsubashi University, Kinokuniya Bookstore, 1970).

but it may not always be possible to satisfy the requirements
for specialized services within the same prefecture. The choice
of location of complementary industries will be particularly important for the reduction of regional inequalities. In the case of
Japan, when heavy industries were located fairly close to major
industrial centers such as Tokyo or Osaka, the ratio of income to
gross value added was much lower: many of the benefits of large-
scale projects were leaking outside the prefecture back to Tokyo.

Another important finding is that, when the regional differential in income per employed workers was broken down into an
industrial composition effect and a residual characterizing the
region, there remained extremely large productivity differentials in
a ratio of 2.8 to 1 between Tokyo prefecture and the poorest
prefecture of Kagoshima. In addition to a size effect for firms
related to location, these productivity differentials underline the
correlation between productivity and city size.

In both the rural and the industrial examples, the channels
for transmitting economic impulses have been shown to be
essential for the narrowing of regional income differentials, and
the local multiplier effects were limited by the absence of complementary economic activities in the region. In the case of the
Muda project, the transmission of economic impulse via the inter-
industrial structure was less important than the effects generated
by household consumption of large amounts of noncompetitive
imports. Additional transfers of resources to other regions were
also made by businesses, and the fiscal structure in Malaysia simply made the situation worse. In the case of Japan, it appears that
interindustry effects and transfers of funds by large firms were
important factors in limiting regional income equalization. It is
quite possible that, over the long run, the necessary complementary activities will locate close to the original large-scale
project, but this adjustment is not automatic, and it will require
direct, detailed, region-specific attention to attract additional
activities.

5

Appropriate National
Urbanization Strategies

The most crucial prerequisites for an effective national urbanization strategy are political commitment at the highest level and appropriate adjustments of the governmental structure and modes of operation. To the extent that government decisionmakers are interested in the spatial outcome of their decisions, there are good chances that the process of learning by doing will lead to increasingly appropriate strategies and policies. A commitment to better policies for urbanization is likely to bring greater convergence and interaction between the implicit effects of national policies, explicit spatial policies, and policies addressed to the problems of the largest cities.

Basic Considerations

At present, two of the three major elements of a national urbanization strategy are not found within the usual framework of national spatial policymaking. First, problems of congestion, pollution, internal city inefficiency, and biased distribution of services among residents should be addressed directly. The joint consideration of national spatial and intraurban policies would greatly clarify the objectives of both sets of policies and the institutional structures required to implement them. Attempts to rely on direct control of the population of the capital region are a particularly poor way of dealing with its internal inefficiencies: Where are all those people supposed to go? Second, the implicit spatial biases in national economic and sectoral policies should be reviewed and addressed directly. Efforts should be made to keep national economic policies and regulations more neutral; policies

129

biased against the rural sector are a good place to start. The improvement of national policies at the margin depends on the national context. To the extent that behind every government policy bias there is a pressure group growing stronger because of it, commitment to better urbanization policies at the highest level is an important requirement for progress.

Direct national spatial policies, which are the third and most familiar area of a national urbanization strategy, have two roles. First, the provision of transport and communication infrastructure is crucial to releasing the growth potential of every region of the country. Second, by improving the comparative advantage of other areas, direct spatial policies help direct migration and resource flows away from the primary city. Great attention must be paid to the transport corridors and urban locations that are likely to channel this growth. It is unlikely that all peripheral regions will be equally attractive at any given time, and the scheduling of government programs must be carefully timed in the light of anticipated national and sectoral economic growth patterns.

In the formulation of national urbanization strategies, a few basic lessons learned from past experience should be kept in mind:

— Spreading resources over all regions and cities is not likely to be effective; pressures to do so are most easily resisted in strong, centralized governments.
— The problems of lagging or depressed regions must be addressed on the basis of their specific growth potential (agriculture, natural resources, or tourism and recreation). In many countries, the cities of such regions do not possess the necessary scale for agglomeration economies; because the poorest regions also have the least developed urban systems, the timing of investment becomes important.
— The scale of national spatial strategies is not uniform. Very large countries such as Brazil and India should emphasize state-level policies once the unintended spatial effects of national policies have been well understood and, it is hoped, improved. In Central America and the Caribbean the problems are almost those of a large metropolitan region and its immediate hinterland.
— In most cases, new towns are wasteful and inefficient ways of approaching the problems of rapid urban growth; satellite

towns within the commuting zone of large cities or company towns are a different matter.

— A spatial strategy that can emphasize intermediate-size cities (scaled according to each country) and major transport corridors will be building from a position of strength.

— Planning for any area cannot be done effectively in isolation. It must be part of a national strategy and based on the comparative advantage of the region as well as a realistic appraisal of national resource constraints.

Stop-and-go policymaking is particularly destructive in the case of national urbanization policies. In the absence of a stable, long-term, coherent national growth policy and of an equally stable spatial policy, the observed patterns of industrial location and individual migration will cause economic activities to concentrate in the largest metropolitan regions. Both the sensible industrialist and the young household will minimize the probability of bankruptcy or unemployment by locating in the largest and richest market: the capital region. The combined effect of an active growth strategy and a consistent national urbanization strategy can convince a business firm that opportunities outside the capital region are meaningful, given very infrequent decisions on business location. In market or mixed economies government instability will render decentralization policies totally ineffective and jeopardize other elements of the national urbanization strategies.

Policy Measures

The many policy measures available for the implementation of national urbanization strategies could be ordered in various ways. First, they could be classified according to their significance for each of the three dimensions of a national urbanization strategy. Policies could also be classified according to the economic sectors they affect: directly productive sectors, such as manufacturing or agriculture; economic overhead sectors, such as transport, energy, telecommunication, or industrial water supply; or human resource sectors, such as education or public health. Another dimension of national urbanization policy measures is their economic character: taxation policies, subsidies, direct public investment, regulation of economic activities, and licensing.

For purposes of policy formulation, it is best to consider the
scale of operation of policy measures, the opportunities at various
levels of decisionmaking, and the level at which specific policies
are most effectively administered.

The level of operation of national urbanization policy measures,
their nature, and their effects are summarized in table 16. Beginning with international policies, the growth strategy of a country
is very important: whether it is export-led or autarkic will influence the nature and location of leading sectors. Trade regulations and tariffs, because they favor certain sectors over others,
also afford preferential treatment to the cities and regions in
which these sectors are predominantly located. International transport policies and participation in shipping conferences can favor
certain coastal zones and specific harbors over others. In some
countries, particularly in Africa and the Middle East, international
migration can have important consequences for both countries
of origin and of destination, since immigrants tend to locate in
large cities.

At the national level, population policies have been listed as a
reminder of their implicit dominance in national urban development; in practice, they are a datum for national urbanization
strategies. Of the other policies listed, those which improve
communication networks are extremely important. Policies that
promote the growth of large private and public organizations
capable of branching out into every city and that foster the
regional and local expansion of business and professional associations are too often overlooked. The rapid diffusion of innovation
and the development of extensive regional networks of information should be strongly encouraged.

The provincial or state level of government is usually called
upon to execute the nationally formulated strategies. In addition,
provincial decisionmakers can identify for the central government
the priorities and appropriate policies for their region. The degree
of actual autonomy exercised at this level of government varies
according to the structure of intergovernmental relations in the
country and, particularly, on the level of fiscal resources actually
controlled by the region. Intergovernmental transfers are always
a problem because the lagging regions most in need of help also
have the weakest resource base.

At the city level, as I have already stressed, internal policies must be appropriate. The quality of city management strongly influences the attractiveness of the location for business firms and the growth potential of the city. Many regulatory methods can either encourage or discourage producers and eventually expand or reduce the resource base of the city. The various aspects of local government that affect the efficiency of a city and the fair treatment of its residents are discussed in detail by Linn.[1]

Provincial governments are typically the main providers of assistance to rural communities. Given the strategies pursued at the national level for the farm sector, they can strongly influence the regional growth of the institutions serving rural populations.

Dominant Policy Issues in Various Countries

Many developing countries are limited market economies at early stages of urbanization. They are urbanizing rapidly because of rapid population growth combined with rural-urban migration flows that are large in relation to the size of the urban system. Their national urban structure is marked by the coexistence of several distinct regional settlements systems which are relatively simple and are being transformed into a single system. The system is not fully integrated since these countries have only recently gained their independence.

Limited Market Economies

For such countries, efforts at deconcentration are probably very premature: concentration of economic activity and population around the leading centers is necessary to maximize the use of scarce managerial resources and skilled labor, given the low level of income. Major urban regions are also the only ones to offer sufficient market density for many light manufacturing activities. But the likelihood that further concentration may be stimulated by inappropriate rural sector policies should not be overlooked.

---

1. Johannes Linn, *Cities in the Developing World: Policies for Their Equitable and Efficient Growth* (New York: Oxford University Press, forthcoming).

Table 16. *Policy Measures for National Urbanization Strategies*

Scale of operation	Nature of policy measures	Effects
Relations with the international economy	Growth strategy and export orientation, foreign exchange policies, tariffs and trade protection, regulation of foreign investments, international transport policies, and immigration and emigration policies.	Most of these policies have implicit effects on the urban system and can accentuate concentration in the largest cities.
National economy	Population policy; public sector investment allocation; intergovernmental fiscal relations, fiscal transfers, and taxation; transport policies (pricing and regulation of various modes and tariffication by product); communication policies (structure of information networks); national growth policy and sectoral priorities; treatment of the rural sector (terms of trade); labor policy (minimum wage legislation and regulation of professions); banking and finance policies (regulation of new branches and conditions of operation); education (regional specialization of higher education); and regulation of public utilities.	Of all the national policies, those for population, sectoral priorities, and the rural sector appear to have the strongest implicit effects. The implicit effects of other policies vary significantly from country to country.
Regional, provincial, or state level, including the urban subsystem and rural service centers	Economic development policies (priorities for the region); public investment policies and diversification of activities; formulation of policies by broad areas; public transport policies (priorities for external links and intra-regional network); industrial estates policies	In most countries the regional level of government is responsible for implementing central government policies and has close control over local activity within cities and rural centers. Strategies must be developed for the long-term growth of the region consistent with national trends. Because of

	and other employment location decisions; allocation of health and social services; regional land policies; education (localization of facilities for general and technical education); regulation of urban and nonurban land use; and regulation of utilities.	economies of scale, concentration of investment in selected urban centers must be phased according to long-term objectives.
Urban level, including the daily commuting zone	Local land-use policies for decentralization; regulation of industrial location and service sector; extensive use of land control as part of urban transport policy; environmental regulations (solid waste, water, and sewerage management); choice of site for satellite cities and policies toward low-income neighborhoods; management of local taxation system and locally owned public utilities; enforcement of codes for building design and construction; location of major traffic generators (markets, public libraries, stadiums); location of hospitals and health clinics.	The internal efficiency of cities is an important factor affecting further growth. The application of zoning controls can enforce decentralization. Broad options for further expansion need to be identified and a local strategy established. It must be consistent with the sources of growth of the city.
Rural centers	Most of the policies for the distribution of services in rural centers are determined at the regional level of government. They are directly affected by national policies toward the rural sector and agriculture.	The growth of rural centers is dependent on farm policies, but strengthening rural services is the direct responsibility of government at the provincial level.

In countries at an early stage of development with a low level of
urbanization, radical changes in the system are more possible than
in other types of countries: for example, national transport
investment can strongly modify the present network of settlements. Such changes are heavily dependent on the effectiveness of
the planning system. Haphazard and strongly unbalanced urban
growth could yield a large urban agglomeration, with self-contained
neighborhoods closely resembling a collection of villages, because
income levels are too low for efficient differentiation of urban
activities. The historical experience of more developed countries
shows that, although new patterns can be created during the first
stages of development, they will quickly become a dominant
factor in the national urban structure.

Large, Low-Income Countries

In the large, low-income countries of Asia, the absolute magnitude of the urban sector and its relatively small share of the total
population indicate that the usual urbanization-industrialization
strategies will not be able rapidly to accommodate a growing
population. Two rather distinct strategies should be devised—one
for the rural sector and one for the urban sector. As long as there
is a severe overall resource constraint, however, tradeoffs between
the two sectors will lead to a heavy rural emphasis in national
policies. This does not imply an anti-urban stance on the part of
policymakers: the internal management of the large cities is an
important problem because of the difficulties as well as the size
of the populations. In India, given the large population of the
country, state-level urban strategies are needed particularly in
those states that are already more than 25 percent urban (Gujarat,
Maharashtra, Mysore, Punjab, Tamil Nadu, and West Bengal).
Given the scarcity of urban resources, their efficient economic
allocation should be stressed. In some cases such as Calcutta,
national economic policies have been a major reason for a pro-
longed period of stagnation.

The essential object of national urbanization strategies in large
African countries is to encourage the growth of the agricultural
sector and to provide national infrastructure in a way that supports the hinterland and favors the development of a balanced
(that is, polycentric) system of cities in the future. Given the
low density of effective demand, the scarcity of managerial talent,

and the low level of urbanization, direct policies of decentralization in most African countries represent the wrong approach. It is more urgent to develop the growth potential of the rural sector and eliminate the very unfavorable terms of trade between the rural and the urban sectors that funnel rural-urban migration toward a few major urban centers. These urban centers are growing extremely rapidly and becoming difficult to manage, in spite of their generally moderate size, because of an insufficient institutional structure and a shortage of managerial talent. The question is not one of decentralization, but of avoiding premature urban concentration through more appropriate national sectoral policies in favor of the rural sector. The examples of the Ivory Coast and Tanzania, which have been following different paths but are emphasizing effective rural development, are positive illustrations of the use of such policies. The economic structure of Nigeria does not look very different from that of the other countries when the mineral sector is isolated from the rest of the economy; the added flexibility provided by oil revenues can be used to support an efficient national pattern of settlements.

Middle-Income Countries

In the middle-income countries, policies dealing with city-to-city interactions as well as rural-urban interactions must be considered. Big cities are a problem, particularly in Asia and Latin America. Too frequently, economists from advanced countries argue that, since they have not found significant social costs for large Western (mostly U.S.) cities, there is probably nothing wrong with the growth of very large cities in middle-income countries. This may prove to be a case of extrapolating research findings out of context. The studies of advanced economies suggest two important results: (1) on the one hand, the social and economic costs of congestion and pollution imposed on the very large cities by newcomers are small and represent only a small percentage of the value of the total city output; (2) on the other hand, failure to charge newcomers fully for the congestion and pollution they impose on present residents leads to a large volume of in-migration, in proportion to the total city population, because of the high wage elasticity of labor demand in these cities.

The social and economic costs experienced by large urban areas in developed countries are small because the urban structure

is fully developed. Cities have grown more slowly in these countries than in developing countries, and their growth occurred when
income levels were already high; therefore appropriate infrastructure exists not only in the capital region but also in alternative
cities.[2] In addition, knowledge about pollution and environmental
costs is widely available and increasingly used; significant pollution
controls are enforced so that the market has been adjusting to
them.

Because of market distortions, however, the social costs of very
large cities in middle-income countries will not be small in relation
to their total output. First, there is a great deal of ignorance about
pollution and congestion—or perhaps a lower sensitivity to the
problems because of lower income levels. There are very few
developing countries in which firms are actually compelled to
control (and thus pay for) the pollution that they emit. Second,
because of a severe lack of infrastructure (both physical and socioeconomic), these firms do not have a wide choice of good locations outside the capital region. There is no precise notion of the
losses imposed on various types of firms in middle-income countries by congestion problems in large cities. These losses occur because the firms lack good alternative locations and are therefore
unable to expand sufficiently to reap full economies of scale.
Meanwhile, migrants have to go where the jobs are, and they
stream into the largest cities because employment opportunities
are lacking elsewhere.

National urbanization policies for the very large cities of the
middle-income countries should pay much greater attention to
the locational needs of business firms, and of manufacturing
firms in particular. Policymakers need to know more about
various activities to determine which firms need to remain in the
largest cities; which firms could benefit from expansion elsewhere because their growth is now constrained; which activities
can be made routine to such an extent that decentralization is

2. Because cities in developing countries are very large, given their income level,
their level of infrastructure is low. For instance, in Japan only 23 percent of households had access to sewer systems in 1975, because of the very fast growth of its cities.
See Japan Economic Planning Agency, *Economic Plan for the Second Half of the 1970s*
(Tokyo, May 1976), p. 112.

not harmful; and which cities and regions are appropriately endowed with the physical and socioeconomic infrastructure to
attract manufacturing firms. With the rapid growth of the population and of the economy, the increasing costs of congestion and
pollution can induce expanding firms to locate away from the
largest urban centers.

Within the large cities much more vigorous policies against
pollution and congestion must be pursued. Business firms should
pay for the pollution that they discharge in the environment.
Cities should make sure that one mode of transport is not subsidized at the expense of other modes. In particular, because the
number of automobiles is rapidly increasing, the owners should
bear the full cost of the resources (space and infrastructure) they
use and the congestion costs that cars impose on public transport
systems in downtown areas. The equitable provision of urban
services is also a major problem.

In the case of very sharp regional disparities, separate efforts
must be made to improve lagging regional economies. It is not a
good idea to mix policies to decentralize away from the capital
region with active policies to reduce regional inequalities by
forcing firms out of the capital into depressed areas. In such areas
the local market is too small to allow even local firms to grow,
and transport and communication systems are weak. Policies concerning depressed regions should be based on their potential comparative advantage (often agriculture). If a region is too poor in
resources to support the local population, a policy that raised
educational levels would allow migrants to move under better
conditions. A combination of higher local income levels and
migrant remittances may eventually bring the region to a new
threshold by increasing its market size. The additional problems
generated by a highly skewed distribution of farmland require
policy reforms going much beyond national urbanization policies.

In the middle-income countries with high population growth
rates (over 2 percent) and an intermediate level of urbanization
(50 percent), it is not reasonable to expect that the population
growth of the largest cities will stop immediately after the implementation of appropriate national urbanization strategies. The
first indicator of success will be merely a deceleration of the
growth rate and the faster expansion of alternative locations.

Advanced Industrialized Countries

There are two dominant national urbanization problems in advanced market economies. First, because they have reached a mature stage of urbanization, rural-urban migration no longer contributes to the expansion of cities. There is considerable resource mobility within the system, and both business firms and highly urbanized migrants are sensitive to the level of amenities offered by different cities.[3] Many very large cities face the new experience of a declining resource base and are still searching for new policy directions based on much stricter allocative efficiency of local resources. As noted earlier, the population decline of the core region is widespread among these countries.

The second important problem of many advanced market economies is the need to adjust to shifts in their international comparative advantage. Some of their industrial sectors have lost their competitive edge against the output of middle-income countries. Structural adjustments are often politically and economically difficult, however, because they affect activities such as steel or textiles which are concentrated in a few well-defined cities or small regions. Adjustment problems seemingly minor in terms of aggregate figures suddenly become difficult; the only thing certain is that postponement of the necessary adjustments will make the transition even more difficult.

3. See, for instance, a recent survey of the Joint Economic Committee of the U.S. Congress reported in "Quality of Life Seen as Crucial by Firms in Assessing Cities," *Wall Street Journal,* January 15, 1979.

APPENDIX A

National Urbanization Policy in Latin America

Even though all Latin American countries share a propensity toward concentration in large cities (see figure A-1), there are important differences in patterns of development among countries. The contrast in settlements patterns between Central America and Mexico, on the one hand, and South America, on the other, has often been pointed out. In Central America the main population centers are in the interior, and the coastal areas are only sparsely settled because of their inhospitable climate. In South America the most densely populated areas and the largest cities are located within a rather narrow fringe on the coast. This coastal pattern of development reflects the historical dependence of the economies on overseas markets for the export of raw material in exchange for industrial goods and new technology. Now, however, the exploitation of natural resources and the strong influence that this exerts on the location of the population are modifying this pattern. Redistribution of population can be stimulated by various resources: in Mexico the development of new oil resources in the Southeast (Tamaulipas, Vera Cruz, Tabasco, and Chiapas) is having a profound effect on the current and prospective structure of settlements patterns in the entire eastern region of the country, as far north as the U.S. border.

Related to the exploitation of natural resources away from the major urban centers and the degree of national integration is the crucial role of transport policies. Internal as well as international integration requires better links between major economic centers and the opening up of the interior, which will considerably affect the existing pattern of settlements. In South America the problem is one of expansion toward the interior; in Central America and

Mexico, where the main economic centers are located along the north-south transport axis, improving national integration requires extending the transport system to the coastal regions.

The geography of South America and the present distribution patterns of population, production, and consumption will dictate the form of economic integration which will be feasible both within and between countries. Topography and climate combined have been an important deterrent to transport development. Frequently a complex structure of mountains makes road building difficult and expensive; elsewhere, the great Amazonian region—the largest tropical rain forest in the world—presents obstacles of a very different kind.

To simplify the description of South America, five major regions can be distinguished according to their major physical, economic, and urbanization characteristics. The first region would be the dominant industrial and urban center of the subcontinent, which covers the southern coastal part of Brazil from Belo Horizonte in the north to Porto Alegre in the south and narrows farther south along the coast to Uruguay and Montevideo. Then comes the urban core of Argentina, with Buenos Aires, Rosario, and Bahia Blanca. A second region would be the hinterland of the urban industrial core, which extends west to the Andes and north to the Amazon Basin. It includes the region of Patagonia, the North Argentinian plateau, the Brazilian *Sertao* and, farther north, the *campo cerrado*, mixed with forest. It also includes part of Uruguay and the entirety of Paraguay, with its rich hydroelectric potential in the east.[1] On the other side of the Andes, Chile would form by itself a third region, uniquely shaped (4,200 kilometers long and 400 kilometers wide), with most of its population clustered in the central region and heavily urbanized. Peru and Bolivia constitute a distinct fourth region, sharply differentiated into a coastal zone and a highland area populated largely by Indians of particularly low standards of living, poorly integrated into the national economy. The *Altiplano* in the center of the continent is a barrier to both domestic and international integration because access to the region is difficult. Farther north, Colombia and Venezuela form a fifth region characterized by geographic homo-

---

1. Alfredo Gutierrez and others, *Paraguay: Regional Development in Eastern Paraguay*, A World Bank Country Study (Washington, D.C., August 1978).

Figure A-1. Urban Concentration in Cities of More than 250,000 in Latin America

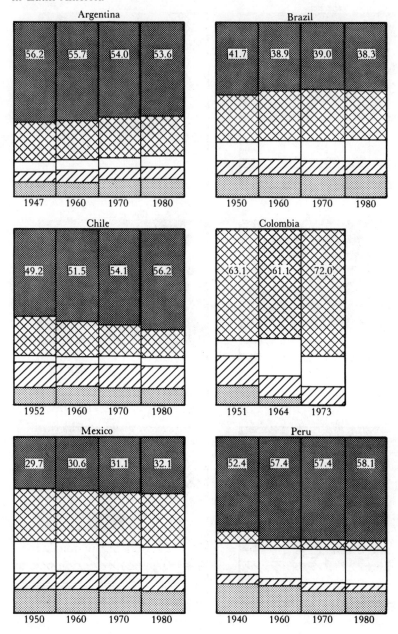

(Figure continues on the following page.)

Figure A-1 *(continued)*

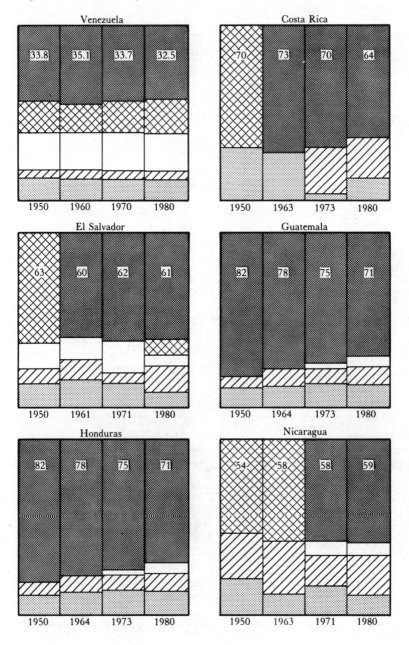

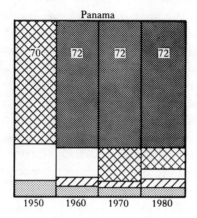

Panama

1950   1960   1970   1980

Note: The numbers on the graph indicate percentages. Latin American countries, except Colombia and Central America, are grouped according to population as follows:

▦ 20,000–50,000

▨ 50,000–100,000

☐ 100,000–250,000

◈ 250,000+

◼ Capital cities or including the largest city.

Colombia is grouped as:

▦ 30,000–50,000

▨ 50,000–100,000

☐ 100,000–250,000

◈ 250,000+

Central American countries, including Panama, are grouped as:

▦ 10,000–20,000

▨ 20,000–50,000

☐ 50,000–100,000

◈ 100,000–250,000

◼ 250,000+

Sources: For Latin American countries, except Colombia and Central America, see Robert W. Fox, *Urban Population Growth Trends in Latin America* (Washington, D.C.: Inter-American Development Bank, 1975), tables 13–18.

For Colombia, see Michael E. Conroy, "Urbanization, Internal Migration, and Spatial Policy in Colombia," World Bank Report no. 1154-CO (Washington, D.C., 1976), table A-1.4.

For Central American countries, including Panama, see Robert W. Fox and Jerrold W. Huguet, *Population and Urban Trends in Central America and Panama* (Washington, D.C.: Inter-American Development Bank, 1977), tables 14–21.

geneity and relative isolation from the rest of the continent by
land because of the Amazon Basin and the Andean mountain
range. Both countries are a mixture of valleys and highlands. In
Colombia, in particular, regional urban centers have blossomed in
the system of separated valleys. Because these regional centers
have not been overwhelmed by the capital, the degree of concentration of urban population in Bogotá is much less than in
other Latin American countries, as can be seen from the index of
primacy (see table 6). The concentration of urban population in
Caracas and the Federal District Miranda is very high in Venezuela,
and projected trends are for even greater concentration.

Ecuador has traits which associate it with Colombia, others
which relate better to Peru and Bolivia. Together with the last
two countries, it has the sharpest division found in Latin America
between the population of European origin and the Indian population. Each group lives in very distinct areas: the mestizo groups
are found along the Pacific coastal areas, while the large, self-
sufficient Indian population lives in the high valleys of the interior.

The Amazon Basin and Northeast Brazil constitute other
natural regions of a distinct character, which have been difficult
to integrate into the national economy of Brazil and the rest of
the continent. The contrast between them is great: while the
Amazon is underpopulated, the Brazilian Northeast has always
had great difficulty in providing employment opportunities to its
population and has been a major source of migration to all other
regions and sectors of the economy. The ten states that make up
the Northeast differ sharply in the size and demographic structure
of their population. The main characteristic of the area is its
undeveloped urban system: there are few very large cities where
activities are concentrated (Salvador, 1,067 million in 1970;
Recife, 1,630 million; Fortaleza, 0.864 million) and many very
small cities of limited importance.

Urbanization and Spatial Development

Spatial development in Latin American countries is characterized by: (1) significant levels of overall development as measured by per capita income, the sophistication of the manufacturing sector, and the productive capacity of the economy; and (2)

conspicuous structural and institutional barriers to the widespread distribution of economic and social progress. Three groups of problems impede development in Latin America: (1) Urban-rural disparities affect the diffusion of economic impulses between urban centers of varying sizes and the region in which they are situated, and the contribution of small and medium-size centers to the rural hinterland surrounding them is particularly limited. (2) Interurban disparities affect the transmission of economic impulses among the various cities in the urban system of each country; these disparities exist throughout the urban hierarchy, among cities of varying sizes, as well as among cities of similar size in various provinces. (3) Interregional disparities have the most immediate repercussions because they affect not only national economic integration but also political and social integration. In the smaller countries of Central America and the Caribbean, an additional problem is that international disparities limit the diffusion of economic growth and hinder their economic integration into more productive and more coordinated systems.

Urban-rural disparities are extremely conspicuous in Latin America. The inequality in landownership patterns has historically yielded a small class of large landowners and extensive absentee ownership (sometimes even based abroad) combined with a large population of tenants, small independent farmers, and laborers. As a result, the population of rural areas has a very low level of education and does not possess the economic and human capital necessary to adopt innovations and raise its level of income. In addition to the generally unstable terms of trade for farm products in the region, the farm population occupied in the production of major export crops, such as coffee, is exposed to the instability of the international markets. In several countries there are strong cultural barriers between the dominant Spanish culture of the large urban centers and the subdued American Indian culture of the countryside. The net effect is that the very pronounced income disparities between cities and rural areas are accompanied by the complete political, sociological, and economic dependence of rural areas on the urban center.

The unequal distribution of land and human capital reduces the ability of rural inhabitants to develop new agricultural methods or to adopt appropriate innovations imported from other regions or other countries. The bias in agricultural research, consistent with the technical needs of the type of farming associated with large landholdings, is a recognized factor in limiting the productivity gains in many Latin American countries. Great inequalities in the distribution of landownership affect patterns of agricultural innovation and deprive the large majority of small-scale farmers from the type of innovation that could raise their income levels, stimulate their regions, and, in turn, greatly improve interactions between small cities and their rural hinterland through product markets as well as factor markets. The situation has been particularly well documented for Argentina but applies elsewhere as well.[2]

Internal spatial development in Latin American countries concerns at least five major types of area:

1. Metropolitan regions, consisting of very large cities or national capitals.
2. Other relatively advanced regions with a level of income higher than the national average. In some the economy is based on manufacturing or mining activities; in others, on rich and productive agriculture.
3. Depressed areas which have a level of income significantly below the national average. The type of action taken in such regions is heavily dependent on the size of the population: in densely populated areas the programs will require much larger investment than in the case of sparsely populated regions, which will of necessity receive much lower priority among national government objectives, except when national security is an issue.
4. New settlement areas. In addition to these first three types of region, which are common everywhere, Latin American countries often have an undeveloped frontier. These new settlement areas have great potential that remains only partially evaluated. In some new settlements, income levels are already fairly high, the promise of further growth fairly clear, and expectations for substantial progress are widespread and attracting private initiatives; in other settlements, income levels are still low, and public sector efforts on

2. Alain de Janvry, "A Socioeconomic Model of Induced Innovations for Argentine Agricultural Development," *Quarterly Journal of Economics*, vol. 87, no. 3 (August 1973), pp. 410-35.

a substantial scale might be required to attract more private efforts into the region.

5. Border areas, such as the new industrial zones in Mexico. (See the following section, which summarizes regional planning efforts in Latin America until the middle 1970s.)

Regional Policies

Since the early 1960s, practically all governments in Latin American countries have created programs of some sort to deal with spatial development either for selected individual regions or for several regions at the same time in a coordinated fashion. Often in the 1970s these plans led to the formulation of national plans such as the recently released National Plan for Human Settlements in Mexico. At the end of the 1960s a survey organized by the Economic Commission for Latin America (ECLA) identified some seventy-five significant regional development programs of various sorts, and the survey was not even an exhaustive one. While some of these reported efforts proved to be ephemeral, others have reached international visibility.[3]

These programs could be classified according to the institutional arrangements created to structure them, according to the method of policy formulation adopted, or according to the nature of the dominant task. Some programs received important powers and had an executive structure to perform a full range of activities, from planning to actual decisionmaking for carrying out the plan. They are generally autonomous organizations, structured as regional corporations, such as Sudene in Brazil, Corporacion de Valle del Cauca in Colombia, Comision del Papaloan in Mexico, and Conzuplan and Corporacion Venezolana de Guyana in Venezuela.

More frequently, commissions, councils, or planning offices have only advisory functions and no executive powers. Because there is no devolution of power and they generally have very limited autonomous financial resources, if any, these coordinating organizations are less conspicuous and probably less effective. A third variety of regional planning effort consists of a noninstitu-

3. This section is essentially based on the very useful study by Walter Stohr, *Regional Development: Experiences and Prospects in Latin America* (Paris and The Hague: Mouton, 1975), especially chap. 2.

tionalized program to coordinate the activities of several sectoral decisionmaking centers directed toward a specific spatial objective, such as a national growth-center policy. In this case, investment policies for energy, transport, and industrial location are expected to favor selected cities within a given size range.

The institutional arrangement chosen affects the origins of policy formulation and executive decision. In some cases the region itself is expected to originate new objectives and specific plans, in other cases central and regional entities cooperate in the effort. Sometimes objectives and criteria are selected solely at the national level.

In a purely regional context, a wide range of major objectives can be used to classify the various programs. This classification is not a rigorous one but is commonly accepted and can always be revised as needed. For Latin American countries, Stohr considered the following dominant objectives: devolution of power and decentralization of decisionmaking; development of depressed regions; new settlements based on agricultural development; new settlements based on mineral resources; development and restructuring of major metropolitan regions; consolidation of other developed areas; development of new growth poles; border area development; and river basin development. Obviously each objective must be related to a characteristic of the country, and more than one dominant objective for national spatial policy may have to be selected. Also, some objectives may be related, but the underlying reasons may differ from country to country.

In the case of devolution and decentralization of decisionmaking, the Brazilian needs differ markedly from those of, say, Bolivia or Chile. In the case of Brazil, the sheer size of the country and of its population requires that decisionmaking be decentralized. In Bolivia or Chile, however, decentralization is needed because of the extreme concentration of decisionmaking power and fiscal resources. Practically all public expenditures are made by the central government, and this concentration of power has paralyzing effects on local initiative, local management, and the timely processing of new projects.

The need to correct wide regional disparities is especially evident in Guatemala and Peru, where the gap between the income level of the capital region and that of the poorest Indian population is very wide. In the case of Mexico, the issue of regional disparities is not so much that the difference between the poorest and the richest region is extreme, but that a very large proportion of the population in the regions earns less than half the national average. In Mexico regional disparity involves several different states and requires a more coordinated set of national policies.

Among the countries with very sparsely populated regions, Paraguay, where the greatest proportion of the national territory is uninhabited, will require policies toward the resource frontier different from those of Uruguay, Venezuela, or Brazil. In Paraguay new policies have to be based on the rapid expansion of the eastern agricultural frontier, combined with major opportunities for border area development near Brazil and Argentina, thanks to the large hydroelectric potential of the Parana River.[4] In Venezuela the development of the Guyana region is based on the exploitation of mineral resources and has called for the the most vigorous effort of this type in Latin America. In Uruguay the development of the agricultural frontier would be aimed at a better distribution of population, which is now almost entirely concentrated in the capital region of Montevideo.

Projects to restructure major metropolitan regions will be quite different, depending on whether they deal with a high concentration of population in the capital region of small countries such as Uruguay, Guatemala, Panama, El Salvador, and most of the Central American as well as the Caribbean countries, or with problems of metropolitan management in the context of large states and vast hinterland regions in countries such as Brazil, Mexico, or Argentina.

Country Scale and the Choice of Strategy: State Policy in São Paulo, Brazil

In addition to the level of urbanization of a country, the size of the area and the population to be subjected to a national settlements planning effort are major considerations. Among the Central American and Caribbean countries the domestic economies are often too small to provide the necessary scale for significant manufacturing activities and room for expansion. Their patterns

---

4. Gutierrez and others, *Paraguay: Regional Development in Eastern Paraguay*.

of urbanization are dependent on the dynamics of their economic growth, which is itself dependent on the strength and stability of international integration schemes. Similar problems are emerging or will be emerging soon for the smaller African countries.

At the other extreme are very large countries which have space so differentiated that problems of national settlements are more effectively addressed at the state level than at the national level. Such countries need a hierarchy of "nested" strategies, whereby general directions for spatial strategy would be given at the national level through the choice of sectoral economic policies and mechanisms for intergovernmental fiscal transfer, but the detail of more specific tactics and the application of instruments would be left to state units. In very large countries the structures of the urban systems are too sharply differentiated between states to permit centralized treatment, and the central government would be too removed from the factual context to guide effectively the details of the policy. Two particularly clear illustrations of the need for nested national settlements strategies are India and Brazil. India's policies are determined by its level of urbanization and the extreme scarcity of resources. Among middle-income countries, Brazil is particularly interesting, and the problems of its Northeast have often been discussed. To illustrate the need for differentiated national settlements policies for subunits and the nature of the spatial dualism that prevails in many middle-income countries, the case of São Paulo is briefly discussed here.

By international standards, the state of São Paulo would rank as an important country by itself. Its population of 23 million represents 21 percent of the population of Brazil. Its gross product of about US$57 billion represents 42.7 percent of the Brazilian GNP. Its contribution by sector represents 55 percent of the industrial output, 35 percent of services, 18 percent of agriculture, and US$4.5 billion (or 38 percent) of all Brazilian exports. Its per capita GNP of US$2,400 is about double the national average. The concentration of human resources in the state is also high, with ten universities spread over 100 campuses claiming about 85 percent of all students working for advanced degrees in Brazil. The state is the financial center of the country: of the forty-seven private banks of the country, twenty-nine have their headquarters in the city of São Paulo. It is estimated that 50 percent of all bank deposits in Brazil are made in the state. Similar statistics con-

cerning the transport, energy, and industrial sectors can be mar-
shaled to illustrate the strong dualistic nature of the national
spatial system of Brazil. The fact that São Paulo exports 68
percent of all Brazilian coffee well illustrates the tendency for the
most dynamic agriculture to be located in the zone of influence
of major urban centers.

The urban system of the state consists of a fully developed
hierarchy of cities with an urban population of more than 12
million, which is still growing in 37 of the 571 municipalities
found in the state. The city of São Paulo, one of the five largest
metropolitan regions of the world, has 59 percent of the urban
population of the state and 10 percent of Brazil's population.
Hence, there is a strongly felt need for a deconcentration strategy
at the state level.

In 1972 São Paulo created "Projects Counter," an advisory
service for firms wishing to establish new industrial plants in the
state. It is meant to coordinate public development with business
requirements. It advises businesses in the choice of alternative
locations in the state, provides technical advice on the tax and
financial incentives available from the federal government through
the Industrial Development Council, and under certain conditions
will even provide financial plans for a project. It is estimated that
in the first five years of operation this program was involved in
planning sites for 300 industrial projects and about half as many
financing arrangements. But this arrangement was deemed clearly
insufficient to bring about significant deconcentration. If it is to
affect the distribution of new economic activities, the state must
show its "visible hand" in a strong and durable fashion to minimize risk for both firms and migrant households.

In 1976 the Regional and Urban Development Policy (PDUR),
was adopted for the deconcentration and decentralization of
industry out of the greater São Paulo region. The central objective of the plan is to demonstrate a commitment to industrial
dispersion to medium-size cities and to improve living conditions
and employment opportunities in these cities and, thus, to increase the choices of urban location by both urban migrants and
business firms. Forty of the 534 municipalities outside the São
Paulo metropolitan region have been selected as strategic locations and should benefit from additional public sector investment
in roads, water and sewage systems, energy supplies, new schools,

and comparable projects. These municipalities are also expected
to undergo a managerial reorganization in order to implement
these plans and to benefit from federal and state funding. This
reorganization would include drawing up a municipal plan, creating municipal planning agencies, comprehensively reviewing local
land use regulations, and reorganizing the tax collection system.
The forty cities have about 16 percent of the total population,
12 percent of the state industrial product, and 12 percent of the
industrial labor force.

The programs are differentiated further according to the region
in which the stategic cities are located and the special needs of the
area:

— *Restoration of the quality of life.* In the metropolitan region
of São Paulo and the Santos coastal zone, growth is to be
controlled to prevent further deterioration of the urban
environment.

— *Controlled expansion.* In the area close to greater São Paulo
(Campinas, Sorocaba, the north coast, and the Rio-São Paulo
area), development is to be controlled strictly to avoid rapid
and chaotic expansion.

— *Dynamic action.* An area farther up-state is expected to be
more effectively connected to São Paulo and to benefit from
new industrial districts and industrial estates, new roads,
housing and water, and waste disposal systems.

— *Promotion.* The southwestern part of the state (western
Paranapanema region and the southern Riberia Valley) is
going to specialize in agribusiness activities. Its prospects
may be greatly improved indirectly by the hydroelectric
projects along the Parana River of more direct value to the
states of Parana and Paraguay.

Work is also in progress for a program to control the process of
urbanization and safeguard scenic areas along the axis between
São Paulo and Rio de Janeiro. This would be done through the
coordination of all government programs.

This São Paulo state program is a good illustration of a national
settlements strategy defined and applied within a subunit of a
country. Success will be a function of the government's ability to
maintain the same strategy over a long time and to solve the problems of resource allocation. Public investment needs to be divided

between the urgent, current needs of the São Paulo urban region, which is developing in an uncontrolled way, and the longer-term needs of the areas of deconcentration. By comparing the sizes of the two budgets, one for the metropolitan region and the other for the medium-size cities, business firms will estimate the state commitment to the urban strategy it has announced and, hence, the degree of risk in selecting the more dispersed locations offered by the new PDUR. The extent to which PDUR's selection of medium-size cities is consistent with the way economic impulses travel through the urban network will also have a major effect.

At the national level the federal government has confronted the problems of the Northeast and the development of the Amazonian frontier through efforts such as SUDENE[5] and the Participation Fund. Brazil has been more successful than many other middle-income countries in creating a cooperative system between the federal and state governments to develop more effective national settlements strategies. More recently, a new legal framework has been created to deal with the problems of metropolitan development on a national scale (Lei Complementar 14 to the 1967 Constitution). The basic principles for an urban policy were defined in the second National Development Plan (1974), and the National Commission on Metropolitan Regions and Urban Policies (CNPU), with resources coming from a new National Urban Development Fund (FNDU), is expected to disburse approximately US$2 billion over the 1975-79 period. Many issues remain to be sorted out, particularly the reconciliation of the effects of sector policy objectives, and their differentiated impact on various states, with the objectives of the national settlements strategies.

5. Superintendencia do Desenvolvimento do Nodeste (Federal Agency for the Development of the Northeast).

APPENDIX B

Urbanization in Large Centrally Planned Economies: The Soviet Union and China

The patterns of urbanization experienced by centrally planned economies are quite different from those of other countries and demonstrate the powerful influence of the political and economic planning system on the type of urbanization that can be achieved. The example of the Soviet Union is discussed first because it is one of the two leading centrally planned economies and its urbanization is easily documented. Further comparative analysis with the other centrally planned economies will confirm the characterizations presented here.

The record shows that, at the beginning of the century, the Soviet Union had about the same level of urbanization as India, with 10 percent of the population urbanized. In 1950 its level of urbanization was almost 40 percent. Since then, the pace of urbanization in the Soviet Union has been higher than that of all the other major U.N. regions of the world. By 1975 it had passed the 60 percent level. This rapid rate of urbanization was caused by large increases in the urban population and a decline in the rural population. The overall population growth rate has been low by world standards (less than 1 percent). During the third quarter of the century, the urban population of the Soviet Union doubled from about 71 million to 154 million. It is remarkable that, in 1950, only 11 percent of the Soviet urban population lived in large cities of more than 1 million. Despite a projected increase in the number of such cities from two in 1950 to twenty-eight by 1985, the share of the population living in large cities is expected to be less than 25 percent at that time—a level still considerably lower than that of most countries. That the Soviet Union had the

Table B-1. *Growth of Cities of More than 1 Million in the Soviet Union*

Item	1950	1960	1970	1975	1980	1990	2000
Number of cities	2	5	10	12	23	29	33
Population (thousands)	7,464	11,954	21,105	25,273	39,288	53,456	65,944
Percent of urban population	10.5	11.4	15.4	16.4	22.8	25.4	26.9
Level of urbanization	39.4	44.3	49.0	60.5	64.2	70.8	76.3

Source: Data provided by the United Nations, Population Division, Department of Economic and Social Affairs.

highest rate of urbanization of the nine broad regions defined by the U.N. Population Division shows that centrally planned economies will not necessarily be more successful in slowing rural-urban migration flows than market economies. The lesser concentration of populations in the very large cities does, however, need explanation. How did the Soviet Union establish such a record when it had pioneered the emphasis on heavy industrialization as the key to development (to the relative neglect of the rural sector) and when this type of strategy has generated elsewhere a heavy concentration of the urban population in the largest cities?

To be specific about the patterns of urbanization in the Soviet Union, table B-1 shows the projected significance of cities of more than 1 million to the end of the century. The Soviet Union appears to be controlling the growth of its very large cities better than most other countries. The methods used have been: (1) a capital-intensive approach to industrial investment combined with a labor-intensive approach to agricultural investment, which has not discouraged the aggregate rural-urban transfer of population; (2) a tendency to limit both investment in infrastructure and the supply of public services, which may have made smaller cities more livable than the large cities; (3) an emphasis on "new" industrial cities, which has concentrated the supply of new services and skilled labor in intermediate urban centers; and (4) the Marxist dogma that the service sector is basically "unproductive" and should be discouraged—another fact that may have played against the rapid growth of the large cities.

The Soviet urban planning ideology has been described as follows:

The works of Marxism-Leninism classics not only justify the necessity of eliminating the antagonism between town and

country and their consequent fusion, but they also outline
how this can be achieved: (1) the harmonious development of
productive forces according to a single overall plan; (2) a greater
equalization of the distribution of large-scale industry and of
the population over the country; (3) achieving strong internal
links between industrial and agricultural production; (4) the
development of communications; (5) overcoming the excessive
concentration of population in large cities (as the capitalist
means of production is eliminated). Socialism will lead to "a
new settlement pattern of mankind with the elimination of both
rural neglect, isolation from the world, its barbarism, and of the
unnatural concentration of huge populations in the large
towns."[1]

It is not at all evident that the Soviet "experience suggests that the
conflict between an industrial development strategy (which favors
spatial concentration) and a dispersed settlement pattern is not
avoided in a centrally planned economy."[2] In fact, the neglect of
agriculture and collectivization may have undermined the viability
of small towns by suppressing small-scale industries and services
in the Soviet Union.

On the basis of U.N. demographic data, a table similar to the
one for the U.S.S.R. can be built for the People's Republic of
China (see table B-2), which has chosen to emphasize rural development rather than heavy industry as a key to rapid development. Unfortunately, the data for China are almost useless for
determining the effect of an agriculturally oriented growth strategy on the expansion of the large cities. From the numbers available, it appears that China has much more urban concentration
than the Soviet Union at a comparable level of urbanization,
probably because of the much greater density of population in
China irrespective of growth strategy.

The sharply fluctuating share represented by the large cities in
the total urban population casts doubt on the strength of the

1. David G. Khodzhaev and Boris S. Khorev, "The Concept of a Unified Settlement
System and the Planned Control of the Growth of Towns in the USSR," *Geographia
Polonica*, vol. 27 (1973), pp. 43-51.
2. Harry W. Richardson, *City Size and National Spatial Strategies in Developing
Countries*, World Bank Staff Working Paper no. 252 (Washington, D.C., April 1977),
p. 33.

Table B-2. *Growth of Cities of More than 1 Million in the People's Republic of China*

Item	1950	1960	1970	1975	1980	1990	2000
Number of cities	7	17	22	26	31	44	47
Population (thousands,	16,682	37,415	51,576	62,558	93,975	116,672	157,508
Percent of urban population	26.9	30.6	30.8	30.1	37.0	32.5	32.9
Level of urbanization	11.5	18.9	21.7	24.8	28.0	34.7	41.5

Source: United Nations, Population Division, November 1975 estimates. These estimates appear to be questionable.

projections attempted by the United Nations for 1975-2000 on the basis of questionable demographic information. The table fully supports the U.N. insistence that such projections are highly dependent on the original data base and the assumptions made about fertility, mortality, and migration. This U.N. warning *must* be heeded, particularly when a single country such as China is "projected" to have an urban population of 478 million (or 15 percent of the urban population of the world) by the year 2000.

For knowledge of urban development in China, it is necessary to rely on the expertise of a few specialists, and only qualitative statements can be made. Until recently, China had a quasi-autarkic approach to development, and for mostly political reasons its international trade—a common source of urban expansion of developing countries—is extremely tightly controlled.

Until 1957 urban growth had been very rapid in China, and rural-urban migration accounted for about 60 percent of the urban increase. The growth strategy that had been devised to encourage the development of Manchuria (already industrialized under the Japanese)—the expansion of cities in the North, the West, and the hinterland—had failed. In 1958 a new policy was introduced, which has persisted to the present, of developing small and medium-size cities. Small cities are those with a population of up to 300,000 and are not restricted in their growth. Medium-size cities have between 400,000 and 700,000 people and a more controlled growth. Cities with about 700,000 residents are considered large, and their growth is discouraged.

There has been a close correlation between urban and industrial growth. If the rate of urban growth has declined since

1957, so has the rate of industrial growth compared with the 1949-57 period. Like the Soviet Union, China has not achieved industrialization without urbanization. Through very close control of the population and very restrictive migration regulations, however, urban planners have succeeded in combining continued economic growth with a stable or even a declining population in the case of several large cities. The renewed emphasis on rapid economic growth and industrialization under the leadership of Vice-Premier Deng Xiaoping may render the task of controlling growth in large cities considerably more difficult.[3]

3. For a more detailed review of Chinese urban and industrial policies, see Christopher Howe, *China's Economy* (New York: Basic Books, 1977).

APPENDIX C

Problems with New Towns: Some Illustrations

Chandigarh, Punjab, India (1973)

Over 25 years of its life, in spite of rigorous development control enforced on a completely new site, approximately 15 percent of the population of the city lives in industrial settlements which have developed outside the visualized framework of the master plan. Fifty-four percent of the commercial and services enterprises also operate in "non-plan" locations and forms. A considerable amount of land use in the city is contrary to that envisaged in the Master Plan. (Madhu Sarin, "Planning and the Urban Poor: The Chandigarh Experience," Ph.D. dissertation, Development Planning Unit, University of London, December 1975, p. x.)

Brazilia, Brazil (1968)

Can the satellite town provide a better life for dwellers on the outlying urban regions of the Federal District, or is Brazilia destined to be surrounded by what is sometimes termed "slum suburbs"? . . . Initially, many in-migrants of impoverished means came to Brazilia to work. They were forced to live in "Cidade Livre" or "Free City" which was several miles outside the capital. At its height, Cidade Livre was a shanty town of 60,000 inhabitants . . . as it became apparent that Cidade Livre was to become a permanent feature of the urban landscape, its name was changed to Nucleo Bandeirante, and an effort was made to correct some of its greatest deficiencies. Three more satellite towns on the periphery of Brazilia—Taguatinta, Gara, and Sobradinho—were established in an attempt to provide cheap housing, for people who as non-government employees had a low priority for housing in Brazilia. (Glenn Stephenson, "Two Newly Created Capitals: Islamabad and Brazilia," *Town and Planning Review*, vol. 41 [October 1970], p. 325.)

Gwangju New Town, Korea (1971), later renamed and reorganized as Songnam

According to the relocation plan, the phased steps were to involve 20,000 in 1969; 55,000 in 1970; 50,000 in 1971; 75,000 in 1972; and 87,000 in the last year of 1973. But as of 1971, it was believed that 60% of the relocatees had left their lots and either returned to the old towns of Seoul *or moved to the peripheral area of the new town.* In both cases, they created new shanty towns by invading public land. *New invasions in the peripheral areas of Gwangju were worse* than the housing lot situation in the town itself. (Won Kim, "A Study of National New Town Development Policy in Korea," Ph.D. dissertation, Columbia University, 1974, p. 881; emphasis added.)

U.S. New Towns (1978)

When the new communities concept was born during the Johnson administration, the idea behind it was to curb uncontrolled suburban growth with the development of *self-contained,* racially and economically integrated communities. Housing was to range from subsidized units to the upper price levels; stores, industries, offices, schools and parks were also included in the planning.

Thirteen planned communities received federal support in the form of long-term debt financing. *Most were located beyond the outer rings of major cities,* although one, Cedar Riverside, was located in downtown Minneapolis, and another, Soul City, in rural North Carolina.

However, all but a few of those projects turned out to be financial failures. Two weeks ago, the Department of Housing and Urban Development announced a plan to liquidate the unsuccessful ones and try to save the others. (*Washington Post,* Saturday, October 7, 1978; emphasis added.)

APPENDIX D

Comparative Urbanization Data on 124 Countries

The tables presented in this appendix are supplementary to the tabular material and figures in chapter 2.

Table D-1. *Urban-Rural Growth Differential, 1950-70*

Rank	Country	Differential	Rank	Country	Differential
1.	Papua New Guinea	10.35	29.	Ghana	4.26
2.	Singapore	9.72	30.	Mozambique	4.22
3.	Zaire	8.82	31.	Iraq	4.18
4.	Kuwait	7.53	32.	Burundi	4.17
5.	Hong Kong	6.61	33.	Turkey	4.11
6.	Mongolia	6.39	34.	Colombia	4.08
7.	Zambia	6.38	35.	Finland	4.05
8.	Yemen Arab Rep.	6.32	36.	Sweden	4.00
9.	Angola	6.27	37.	Uganda	3.98
10.	Central Africa	6.09	38.	Brazil	3.89
11.	Rwanda	5.99	39.	Rhodesia	3.86
12.	Venezuela	5.90	40.	Madagascar	3.80
13.	Lesotho	5.88	41.	China	3.79
14.	Lebanon	5.85	42.	Dominican Rep.	3.76
15.	Guinea	5.85	43.	Uruguay	3.75
16.	Korea, Rep. of	5.71	44.	France	3.72
17.	Chad	5.61	45.	Japan	3.61
18.	Ivory Coast	5.51	46.	Mauritania	3.55
19.	Ethiopia	5.50	47.	Jamaica	3.53
20.	Algeria	5.35	48.	Congo, People's Rep.	3.52
21.	Bulgaria	5.30	49.	U.S.S.R.	3.48
22.	Nepal	5.17	50.	Canada	3.48
23.	Benin	5.17	51.	Romania	3.47
24.	Cameroon	4.74	52.	Jordan	3.45
25.	Saudi Arabia	4.43	53.	Albania	3.45
26.	Cambodia	4.41	54.	Liberia	3.38
27.	Korea, Dem. Rep.	4.33	55.	Mexico	3.37
28.	Chile	4.27			

(Table continues on following page)

Table D-1 (*continued*)

Rank	Country	Differential	Rank	Country	Differential
56.	Morocco	3.29	92.	Israel	2.18
57.	Afghanistan	3.27	93.	Czechoslovakia	2.15
58.	Yugoslavia	3.27	94.	Nicaragua	2.14
59.	Greece	3.21	95.	Norway	2.14
60.	Argentina	3.18	96.	Germany,	
61.	Upper Volta	3.17		Fed. Rep. of	2.13
62.	Kenya	3.11	97.	Bolivia	2.08
63.	Denmark	3.10	98.	Switzerland	2.08
64.	Burma	3.03	99.	Senegal	2.07
65.	Poland	3.01	100.	Italy	2.04
66.	Niger	2.92	101.	Thailand	1.99
67.	Yemen, People's		102.	Malaysia	1.96
	Dem. Rep.	2.89	103.	Sierra Leone	1.87
68.	Tanzania	2.89	104.	Bangladesh	1.79
69.	Spain	2.89	105.	Syria	1.72
70.	Somalia	2.77	106.	Hungary	1.71
71.	Pakistan	2.68	107.	Australia	1.60
72.	Egypt	2.66	108.	Cuba	1.56
73.	Haiti	2.65	109.	Portugal	1.54
74.	Vietnam	2.65	110.	Belgium	1.47
75.	New Zealand	2.63	111.	Philippines	1.38
76.	Laos	2.60	112.	South Africa	1.30
77.	Nigeria	2.60	113.	Netherlands	1.30
78.	Peru	2.59	114.	India	1.11
79.	Iran	2.59	115.	Bhutan	0.87
80.	Libya	2.58	116.	Honduras	0.86
81.	Sri Lanka	2.57	117.	German	
82.	Sudan	2.55		Dem. Rep.	0.70
83.	Panama	2.55	118.	Costa Rica	0.62
84.	Tunisia	2.50	119.	Paraguay	0.57
85.	Togo	2.38	120.	Guatemala	0.51
86.	Malawi	2.38	121.	Austria	0.51
87.	United States	2.37	122.	El Salvador	0.46
88.	Ecuador	2.34	123.	Trinidad	
89.	Indonesia	2.32		and Tobago	0.32
90.	Ireland	2.26	124.	United Kingdom	-0.41
91.	Mali	2.26			

Table D-2. *Percentage Share of Net Migration in the Growth of the Urban Sector, 1970-75*

Rank	Place	Percent	Rank	Place	Percent
1.	German Dem. Rep.	160.00	44.	France	55.56
2.	Angola	98.39	45.	Burma	54.17
3.	Bulgaria	82.14	46.	Kampuchea	54.10
4.	Uruguay	76.47	47.	Ethiopia	53.57
5.	Yemen Arab Republic	76.25	48.	Morocco	52.94
6.	Germany, Fed. Rep of	75.00	49.	Portugal	52.94
7.	Papua New Guinea	74.26	50.	Jamaica	52.63
8.	Finland	73.68	51.	Uganda	51.47
9.	Hungary	73.33	52.	Congo, People's Rep.	51.11
10.	Rwanda	70.13	53.	Albania	51.02
11.	Belgium	70.00	54.	Ghana	50.91
12.	Yugoslavia	68.97	55.	Bhutan	50.00
13.	Romania	67.86	56.	Niger	50.00
14.	Lesotho	67.16	57.	Yemen, People's Dem. Rep.	50.00
15.	Chad	66.67	58.	Austria	50.00
16.	Sweden	66.67	59.	Denmark	50.00
17.	Burundi	65.57	60.	Laos	48.98
18.	Norway	65.00	61.	Somalia	48.94
19.	Taiwan	64.29	62.	Indonesia	48.94
20.	Nigeria	64.29	63.	China	48.48
21.	Tanzania	64.00	64.	Madagascar	48.33
22.	Cameroon	63.46	65.	Togo	48.00
23.	Korea, Rep. of	63.27	66.	Ireland	47.83
24.	Nepal	62.50	67.	Bangladesh	47.37
25.	U.S.S.R.	62.50	68.	Spain	47.37
26.	Central Africa	62.07	69.	Dominican Rep.	47.27
27.	Saudi Arabia	61.90	70.	Korea, Dem. Rep. of	47.06
28.	Sudan	61.82	71.	United States	46.67
29.	Mozambique	60.06	72.	Mauritania	46.00
30.	Sri Lanka	60.47	73.	Mali	45.65
31.	United Kingdom	60.00	74.	Thailand	45.28
32.	Afghanistan	59.26	75.	Tunisia	45.24
33.	Benin	59.09	76.	India	44.75
34.	Poland	59.09	77.	Kenya	44.44
35.	Greece	58.82	78.	Lebanon	44.44
36.	Czechoslovakia	58.82	79.	Mongolia	44.44
37.	Switzerland	57.89	80.	Algeria	43.86
38.	Zaire	57.81	81.	Egypt	43.59
39.	Guinea	57.58	82.	Vietnam	43.48
40.	Zambia	57.35	83.	Pakistan	43.40
41.	Malawi	56.60	84.	Sierra Leone	43.18
42.	Upper Volta	55.77	85.	Liberia	43.10
43.	Haiti	55.56	86.	Colombia	42.86

(Table continues on following pages)

Table D-2 (*continued*)

Rank	Place	Percent	Rank	Place	Percent
87.	Malaysia	42.55	106.	Singapore	32.00
88.	Trinidad		107.	Australia	31.82
	and Tobago	42.11	108.	Peru	30.95
89.	Philippines	41.67	109.	Canada	30.00
90.	Rhodesia	40.68	110.	South Africa	29.73
91.	Turkey	40.48	111.	Paraguay	27.03
92.	Iran	40.43	112.	Nicaragua	26.67
93.	Honduras	40.00	113.	Panama	26.19
94.	Japan	39.13	114.	Netherlands	25.00
95.	Italy	38.46	115.	Kuwait	24.39
96.	Cuba	37.93	116.	Mexico	23.91
97.	Brazil	35.56	117.	Syria	21.43
98.	Ivory Coast	35.38	118.	El Salvador	20.51
99.	Argentina	35.00	119.	Venezuela	20.51
100.	Jordan	34.69	120.	Guatemala	20.00
101.	Costa Rica	34.21	121.	Libya	16.00
102.	Senegal	34.15	122.	Ecuador	10.26
103.	Iraq	34.00	123.	New Zealand	05.26
104.	Chile	33.33	124.	Israel	02.94
105.	Bolivia	32.50	125.	Hong Kong	-11.76

Table D-3. *Urban and Total Population Growth Rates,*
1970-75, Ranked according to per Capita GNP

Rank	Place	Total population growth	Urban population growth
Low-income			
1.	Bhutan	2.3	4.6
2.	Cambodia	2.8	6.1
3.	Laos	2.5	4.9
4.	Ethiopia	2.6	5.6
5.	Mali	2.5	4.6
6.	Bangladesh	2.0	3.8
7.	Rwanda	2.3	7.7
8.	Somalia	2.4	4.7
9.	Upper Volta	2.3	5.2
10.	Burma	2.2	4.8
11.	Burundi	2.1	6.1
12.	Chad	2.1	6.3
13.	Nepal	2.1	5.6
14.	Benin	2.7	6.6
15.	Malawi	2.3	5.3
16.	Zaire	2.7	6.4
17.	Guinea	2.8	6.6
18.	India	2.1	3.8
19.	Vietnam	2.6	4.6
20.	Afghanistan	2.2	5.4
21.	Niger	2.7	5.4
22.	Lesotho	2.2	6.7
23.	Mozambique	2.4	6.1
24.	Pakistan	3.0	5.3
25.	Tanzania	2.7	7.5
26.	Haiti	1.6	3.6
27.	Madagascar	3.1	6.0
28.	Sierra Leone	2.5	4.4
29.	Sri Lanka	1.7	4.3
30.	Central African Emp.	2.2	5.8
31.	Indonesia	2.4	4.7
32.	Kenya	3.5	6.3
33.	Uganda	3.2	6.8
34.	Yemen Arab Rep.	1.9	8.0
Middle-income		2.7	4.5
35.	Togo	2.6	5.0
36.	Egypt	2.2	3.9
37.	Yemen, People's Dem. Rep.	2.7	5.4
38.	Cameroon	1.9	5.2
39.	Sudan	2.1	5.5
40.	Angola	0.1	6.2
41.	Mauritania	2.7	5.0
42.	Nigeria	2.5	7.0

(Table continues on following pages)

Table D-3 (*continued*)

Rank	Place	Total population growth	Urban population growth
43.	Thailand	2.9	3.3
44.	Bolivia	2.7	4.0
45.	Honduras	2.7	4.5
46.	Senegal	2.7	4.1
47.	Philippines	2.8	4.8
48.	Zambia	2.9	6.8
49.	Liberia	3.3	5.8
50.	El Salvador	3.1	3.9
51.	Papua New Guinea	2.6	10.1
52.	Congo, People's Rep.	2.2	4.5
53.	Morocco	2.4	5.1
54.	Rhodesia	3.5	5.9
55.	Ghana	2.7	5.5
56.	Ivory Coast	4.2	6.5
57.	Jordan	3.2	4.9
58.	Colombia	2.8	4.9
59.	Guatemala	3.2	4.0
60.	Ecuador	3.5	3.9
61.	Paraguay	2.7	3.7
62.	Korea, Rep. of	1.8	4.9
63.	Nicaragua	3.3	4.5
64.	Dominican Rep.	2.9	5.5
65.	Syrian Arab Rep.	3.3	4.2
66.	Peru	2.9	4.2
67.	Tunisia	2.3	4.2
68.	Malaysia	2.7	4.7
69.	Algeria	3.2	5.7
70.	Turkey	2.5	4.2
71.	Costa Rica	2.5	3.8
72.	Chile	1.8	2.7
73.	Taiwan	2.0	5.6
74.	Jamaica	1.8	3.8
75.	Lebanon	3.0	5.4
76.	Mexico	3.5	4.6
77.	Brazil	2.9	4.5
78.	Panama	3.1	4.2
79.	Iraq	3.3	5.0
80.	Uruguay	0.4	1.7
81.	Romania	0.9	2.8
82.	Argentina	1.3	2.0
83.	Yugoslavia	0.9	2.9
84.	Portugal	0.8	1.7
85.	Iran	2.8	4.7
86.	Hong Kong	1.9	1.7
87.	Trinidad and Tobago	1.1	1.9
88.	Venezuela	3.1	3.9

Rank	Place	Total population growth	Urban population growth
89.	Greece	0.7	1.7
90.	Singapore	1.7	2.5
91.	Spain	1.0	1.9
92.	Israel	3.3	3.4
Industrialized		0.8	1.8
93.	South Africa	2.6	3.7
94.	Ireland	1.2	2.3
95.	Italy	0.8	1.3
96.	United Kingdom	0.2	0.5
97.	New Zealand	1.8	1.9
98.	Japan	1.4	2.3
99.	Austria	0.4	0.8
100.	Finland	0.5	1.9
101.	Australia	1.5	2.2
102.	Netherlands	0.9	1.2
103.	France	0.8	1.8
104.	Belgium	0.3	1.0
105.	Germany, Fed. Rep. of	0.2	0.8
106.	Norway	0.7	2.0
107.	Denmark	0.5	1.0
108.	Canada	1.4	2.0
109.	United States	0.8	1.5
110.	Sweden	0.4	1.2
111.	Switzerland	0.8	1.9
Capital surplus oil exporters		4.2	6.3
112.	Saudi Arabia	2.4	6.3
113.	Libya	4.2	5.0
114.	Kuwait	6.2	8.2
Centrally planned economies		0.9	2.8
115.	China	1.7	3.3
116.	Korea, Dem. Rep.	2.7	5.1
117.	Albania	2.4	4.9
118.	Cuba	1.8	2.9
119.	Mongolia	3.0	5.4
120.	Hungary	0.4	1.5
121.	Bulgaria	0.5	2.8
122.	U.S.S.R.	0.9	2.4
123.	Poland	0.9	2.2
124.	Czechoslovakia	0.7	1.7
125.	German Dem. Rep.	−0.3	0.5

Source: World Bank, *World Development Report, 1978* (New York: Oxford University Press, 1978), Annex, table 13, p. 100.

Table D-4. *Four-city Primacy Index for Selected Countries, 1976*

4.000 and over
1. Zaire: 4.047
2. Chile: 4.823

3.000-3.999
1. Peru: 3.376
2. Hungary: 3.741

2.000-2.999
1. Mexico: 2,634 (2.754)
2. Iran: 2.344
3. Austria: 2.783
4. United Kingdom: 2.640
5. Romania: 2.448 (2.208)

1.000-1.999
1. Egypt: 1.642
2. Morocco: 1.261 (1.202)
3. Cuba: 1.463
4. Argentina: 1.546
5. Bolivia: 1.179 (4.063)
6. Colombia: 1.085 (.931)
7. Venezuela: 1.232
8. Burma: 1.881
9. Indonesia: 1.344
10. Iraq: 1.987 (2.183)
11. Japan: 1.523 (1.523)
12. Korea, Rep.: 1.535
13. Vietnam: 1.625
14. Bulgaria: 1.290
15. Czechoslovakia: 1.135
16. Denmark: 1.296
17. Finland: 1.145
18. France: 1.281 (3.377)
19. Greece: 1.331 (1.880)
20. Spain: 1.131
21. Australia: 1.491 (.652)
22. Bangladesh: n.a. (1.143)
23. Algeria: 1.250 (1.256)

0.500-0.999
1. Nigeria: 0.632
2. Sudan: 0.528
3. Canada: 0.770 (0.621)
4. United States 0.979 (0.615)
5. Brazil: 0.810 (1.917)
6. Afghanistan: 0.667
7. China: 0.759
8. India: 0.670
9. Israel: 0.759
10. Malaysia: 0.691
11. Pakistan: 0.968
12. Philippines: 0.746
13. Saudi Arabia: 0.581
14. Syria: 0.863
15. Turkey: 0.976 (1.120)
16. Belgium: 0.541 (0.798)
17. German Dem. Rep.: 0.798
18. Germany, Fed. Rep.: 0.738
19. Italy: 0.690
20. Netherlands: 0.558 (0.484)
21. Poland: 0.697
22. Sweden: 0.824
23. Switzerland: 0.782 (0.726)
24. Yugoslavia: 0.664
25. U.S.S.R.: 0.968
26. Zambia: n.a. (0.574)

Less than 0.499
1. South Africa: 0.386 (0.573)
2. New Zealand: 0.403

n.a. Not available.
Note: The index is the ratio of the largest city over the next three largest. The numbers in parentheses give the index for the functional urban agglomeration as opposed to the largest city as legally defined.
Source: United Nations, *Demographic Yearbook, 1976.*

Table D-5. *Indicators for the Typology of Economies*

Country	1976 GNP per capita (U.S. dollars)	Land area (thousand square kilometers)	Population National (millions)	Population Largest city (thousands)	1976 GNP[a] (millions of U.S. dollars)
MARKET AND MIXED ECONOMIES					
Very small[b]					
1. Hong Kong	2,110	1	4.5	4,010	9,495
2. Singapore	2,700	1	2.3	2,250	6,210
With limited domestic markets					
1. Nepal	120	141	12.9	150	1,548
2. Sri Lanka	200	66	13.8	655	2,760
3. Papua New Guinea	490	462	2.8	113	1,372
4. Afghanistan	160	648	14.0	749	2,240
5. Sierra Leone	200	72	3.1	214	620
6. Mozambique	170	783	9.5	384	1,615
7. Cameroon	290	475	7.6	250	2,204
8. Upper Volta	110	274	6.2	59	682
9. Somalia	110	638	3.3	230	363
10. Mali	100	1,240	5.8	197	580
11. Yemen Arab Rep.	250	195	6.0	120	1,500
12. Niger	160	1,267	4.7	130	752
13. Benin	130	113	3.2	178	416
14. Madagascar	200	587	9.1	378	1,820
15. Chad	120	1,284	4.1	179	492
16. Guinea	150	246	5.7	197	855
17. Rwanda	110	26	4.2	54	462
18. Uganda	240	236	11.9	331	2,856

(Tables continues on following pages)

Table D-5 (continued)

Country	1976 GNP per capita (U.S. dollars)	Land area (thousand square kilometers)	Population National (millions)	Largest city (thousands)	1976 GNP[a] (millions of U.S. dollars)
19. Malawi	140	119	5.2	160	728
20. Togo	260	56	2.3	148	598
21. Burundi	120	28	3.8	79	456
22. Senegal	390	196	5.1	808	1,989
23. Ghana	580	239	10.1	967	5,858
24. Zambia	440	753	5.1	448	2,244
25. Ivory Coast	610	323	7.0	282	4,270
26. Angola	330	1,247	5.5	475	1,815
27. Rhodesia	550	391	6.5	568	3,575
28. El Salvador	490	21	4.1	565	2,009
29. Haiti	200	28	4.7	494	940
30. Jamaica	1,070	11	2.1	605	2,247
31. Dominican Rep.	780	49	4.8	929	3,744
32. Nicaragua	750	130	2.3	385	1,725
33. Paraguay	640	407	2.6	565	1,664
34. Costa Rica	1,040	51	2.0	401	2,030
35. Bolivia	390	1,099	5.8	655	2,262
36. Honduras	390	112	3.0	296	1,170
37. Guatemala	630	109	6.5	979	4,095
Large, low-income					
Africa					
1. Egypt	280	1,001	38.1	6,932	10,668
2. Ethiopia	100	1,222	28.7	1,153	2,870
3. Kenya	240	583	13.8	699	3,312
4. Tanzania	180	945	15.1	517	2,718

		1	2	3	4	5
5.	Nigeria	380	924	77.1	2,064	29,298
6.	Zaire	140	2,345	25.4	2,008	3,556
7.	Sudan	290	2,506	15.9	803	4,611
Asia						
1.	Burma	120	677	30.8	2,449	3,696
2.	India	150	3,288	620.4	8,077	93,060
3.	Indonesia	240	1,904	135.2	5,593	32,448
4.	Pakistan	170	804	71.3	4,465	12,121
5.	Bangladesh	110	144	80.4	1,918	8,844
Middle-income						
Asia						
1.	Philippines	410	300	43.3	4,444	17,753
2.	Korea, Rep. of	670	99	36.0	7,286	24,120
3.	Thailand	380	514	43.0	3,277	16,340
4.	Malaysia	860	330	12.7	452	10,922
5.	Taiwan	1,070	36	16.3	2,023	17,441
Mediterranean and Middle East						
1.	Algeria	990	2,382	16.2	1,179	16,038
2.	Turkey	990	781	41.2	3,255	40,788
3.	Morocco	540	447	17.2	1,856	9,288
4.	Iran	1,936	1,648	34.3	4,435	66,405
5.	Syria	780	185	7.7	1,053	6,006
6.	Tunisia	840	164	5.7	931	4,788
7.	Jordan	610	98	2.8	634	1,708
8.	Iraq	1,390	435	11.5	3,433	15,985
9.	Lebanon	-1	10	3.2	1,243	-1
10.	Spain	2,920	505	35.7	3,520	104,244
11.	Israel	3,920	21	3.6	1,138	14,112

(Table continues on following pages)

Table D-5 (continued)

Country	1976 GNP per capita (U.S. dollars)	Land area (thousand square kilometers)	Population National (millions)	Population Largest city (thousands)	1976 GNP[a] (millions of U.S. dollars)
12. Portugal	1,690	92	9.7	1,278	16,393
13. Greece	2,590	132	9.1	2,764	23,569
14. Saudi Arabia	4,480	2,150	8.6	667	38,528
15. Libya	6,310	1,760	2.5	214	15,775
Latin America (rapid urban population growth)					
1. Ecuador	640	284	7.3	1,006	4,672
2. Peru	800	1,285	15.8	3,901	12,640
3. Colombia	630	1,139	24.2	3,416	15,246
4. Mexico	1,090	1,973	62.0	11,943	67,580
5. Brazil	1,140	8,512	110.0	9,965	125,400
6. Venezuela	2,570	912	12.4	2,673	31,868
Latin America (slow urban population growth)					
1. Chile	1,050	757	10.5	2,850	11,025
2. Argentina	1,550	2,767	25.7	8,436	39,835
3. Uruguay	1,390	178	2.8	1,559	3,892
Advanced industrial					
1. Netherlands	6,200	41	13.8	1,032	85,560
2. Belgium	6,780	31	9.8	1,099	66,444
3. United States	7,890	9,363	215.1	17,013	1,697,139
4. Italy	3,050	301	56.2	6,030	171,410
5. Canada	7,510	9,976	23.2	3,048	174,232
6. Sweden	8,670	450	8.2	1,358	71,094
7. Germany, Fed. Rep.	7,380	249	62.0	9,701	457,560
8. Switzerland	8,880	41	6.4	765	56,832
9. Japan	4,910	372	112.8	17,317	553,848
10. France	6,550	547	52.9	9,863	364,695

No.	Country				
11.	United Kingdom	4,020	244	56.1	10,711	225,522
12.	Australia	6,100	7,687	13.7	2,984	83,570
13.	Finland	5,620	337	4.7	853	26,414
14.	New Zealand	4,250	269	3.1	716	13,175
15.	Denmark	7,450	43	5.1	1,328	37,995
16.	Norway	7,420	324	4.0	663	29,680
17.	Austria	5,330	84	7.5	1,888	39,975
18.	Ireland	2,560	70	3.2	883	8,142
19.	South Africa	1,340	1,221	26.0	1,659	34,840

CENTRALLY PLANNED ECONOMIES

Low-income

No.	Country				
1.	China	410	9,597	865.8	10,888	354,978
2.	Laos	90	237	3.3	132	297
3.	Cuba	860	115	9.5	2,269	8,170
4.	Vietnam	-1	333	47.6	2,046	-1
5.	Korea, Dem. Rep.	470	121	16.3	1,157	7,661
6.	Albania	540	29	2.5	169	1,350
7.	Kampuchea	-1	181	8.1	605	-1

Middle-income

No.	Country				
1.	U.S.S.R.	2,760	22,402	256.7	7,734	708,492
2.	Yugoslavia	1,680	256	21.5	870	36,120
3.	Romania	1,450	238	21.4	1,715	31,030
4.	Bulgaria	2,310	111	8.8	1,091	20,328
5.	Hungary	2,280	93	10.6	2,063	24,168

Higher-income

No.	Country				
1.	German Dem. Rep.	4,220	108	16.8	1,102	70,896
2.	Czechoslovakia	3,840	128	14.9	1,096	57,216
3.	Poland	2,860	313	34.3	3,012	98,098

a. Estimated total GNP is based on the product of the per capita GNP and total population.

b. Only advanced city-states are shown in the table; there are no data listings for small, low-income economies.

Source: World Bank, *World Development Report, 1978* (New York: Oxford University Press, 1978).

Index

Advanced industrialized countries: typology data on, 174-75; urbanization policies and, 50-51, 140

Africa, 43, 136; farm sector in, 92; typology data on, 172-73; urbanization levels and, 18-19; urbanization strategies and, 44-45

Agglomeration process, 85, 107, 130

Agriculture: bias against, 104-05, 130; in centrally planned economies, 52; in Latin America, 147-48; middle-income countries and, 47; policy and, 99; regional investment example and, 125-26; in Soviet Union, 157, 158; transport and, 70, 71. *See also* Farm sector

Algeria, 47

Annexation, 16, 30

Argentina, 29, 49-50, 142; landownership in, 94

Asia, 45, 121; middle-income countries in, 46-47; typology data on, 173; urbanization levels and, 19; urbanization strategies and, 42-43; urban-rural linkages and, 92-93. *See also names of specific Asian countries*

Australia, 22

Bangladesh, 43

Bergsman, Joel, 65

Berry, Brian J. L., 96, 97

Bogotá, 76-77, 90

Bolivia, 142, 150

Border regions, national security and, 99-100. *See also* Regional development; Regional inequalities

Brazil, 27, 49, 71, 99, 102, 130, 142, 146, 150; settlement patterns in, 151-55

Brazilia, 161-62

Brookfield, Harold, 92

Bulgaria, 29

Burma, 43

Business: location choice and, 85-87; mobility patterns and, 59. *See also* Corporations; Firms

Calcutta, 88

Capital regions, 7, 57, 131; advanced economies and, 50; efficiency and, 108; energy prices and, 105; limited domestic market countries and, 42-43; location choices and, 86; migration and, 88, 89, 90; national economic structure and, 102; new towns and, 115

Caribbean island economies, 42, 130

Central America, 42, 130

Centrally planned economies, 39; settlement policies and, 51-53; spatial development and, 38; typology data on, 175; urbanization and, 22, 31, 156-60. *See also* China; Soviet Union

Central-place theory (cities), 61-62

China, 99; settlement patterns in, 51-53; urbanization in, 158-60; urbanization levels and, 19, 26-27

Chile, 29, 49-50, 150

Christaller, Wilhelm, 61

Cities: central-place theory and, 61-62; in China, 159; classification of, 8, 59-60, 66; distance between, 66; economic efficiency and, 110-13; economic growth transmission and, 61-64, 65; efficiency and, 7, 8, 107-08; employment and, 65; expanding or mature urbanization and,

Cities continued.
57-59; in Latin America, 19, 49; location of, 64, 67; location choice constraints and, 83-87; manufacturing and, 64, 65-66; in Middle East, 48; national system of, 100; optimal size of, 56-57; policy and, 133, 137-39; population concentration in large, 31-32; population definition and, 13, 17; primacy and, 32-36, 107-08; provincial, 81-83, 84, 86; size, location, and function of, 59-60; in Soviet Union, 156, 157; transport and, 67-73. *See also names of specific cities*

Classifications: of cities, 59-60; of countries, 39-42; policy measures and, 131-33

Cohen, Monique, 92

Colombia, 49, 69 n.18, 71, 76-77, 142, 146; landownership in, 93; migration redirection and, 89-90

Communications, 7, 68, 86, 120, 121, 130

Corporations, multilocational character of, 63-64. *See also* Business; Firms

Cost of living, 121-23

Countries: classification of, 39-42; comparative urbanization data on, 163-75; urbanization strategies for, 42-53. *See also specific class of countries*

Decentralization, 3, 8, 37, 47, 57, 89; constraints on, 83-87; of decision-making, 150; manufacturing and, 75, 81-83; of Paris and London, 59; policy and, 137, 138-39; transport and, 73

Deng Xiaoping, vice-premier, 160

Dualism, spatial policy and, 116-28

Earnings: minimum wage law and, 105-06; regional transfer of, 63

Economic development: cities and, 65; economic efficiency and, 108-13; integration of, 56; policy measures and, 131-32; transmission of, among cities, 61-64; unintended spatial effects and, 101-07; urbanization levels and, 17

Ecuador, 49, 146

Education, 38, 46, 51, 83, 84, 139

Efficiency: cities and, 7, 8; national economic, 108-13, 116; primacy and, 107-08; transport and, 70

Egypt, 44

Employment, 55, 64; cities and, 65; manufacturing location and, 73, 75, 83; migration and search for, 87-88; new towns and, 115-16; regional planning and, 63; urban labor markets and, 29

English, John, 92

Environmental damage, 110, 138

Ethiopia, 27, 44

Europe, urbanization levels and, 22. *See also names of specific European countries*

European Economic Community, 29

Exports, 132, 147; Brazilian, 152-53; industrial estates (Korea) and, 82-83; Korea and, 37; middle-income countries and, 46-47

Farm sector, 8, 9; landownership and, 94-95; urban interaction with, 91-93. *See also* Agriculture; Rural sector

Fertility, 16, 30, 88, 159

Firms: branch plants and, 81-83; location choice constraints and, 83-87; relocation and, 79-81; transport and, 69 n.18. *See also* Business; Corporations

France, 29, 59

Freight rates, 69-70; tariffs and, 105

Friedmann, John, 117 n.20

Gardner, John, 112

German Democratic Republic, 31, 51

Germany, Federal Republic of, 26

Government, 6; advanced economies and, 50; economic regulations and, 105-06; fiscal resources and, 106-07; industrial estates and, 83; Korean farm sector and, 94-95; policy and, 132; spatial development constraints and, 38; urbanization policies and, 98, 100

Great Britain, 5, 13, 27, 59

Greece, 29, 49

Greenston, Peter, 65

Gross national product (GNP), per capita, spatial development and, 37

Gross regional product (GRP), 117
Growth potential: agricultural bias of
    policy and, 104; regional equality
    and, 121; transmission of economic
    impulses and, 61-64
Growth rates: components of urban,
    29-31; data on population, 167-69;
    income equality and, 119-28; popula-
    tion projections and, 13-15; rural
    population and, 27; urban popula-
    tion and, 16-17, 27
Guatemala, 150, 151

Healy, Robert, 65
Hong Kong, 29, 42; primacy and, 32
Housing, 115
Human resources, 38, 46

Imports, 126
Import substitution, 104
Income, 81, 84, 108, 110, 147, 148; in
    cities, 138 n.2; farm, 92, 93; regional,
    99, 119-28
Income distribution, 37
India, 43, 99, 130, 136, 152; urbaniza-
    tion levels and, 19, 26
Indonesia, 19, 43
Industrial estates, 82-83
Industrialization, 7, 67, 68; in centrally
    planned economies, 52-53; in China,
    158-60; expanding urbanization and,
    57; in Japan, 126-28; population con-
    centration and, 73-87
Industry, 55, 64; bias against agriculture
    and, 104; in centrally planned
    economies, 52; incentives for, 102-
    04; in middle-income countries, 46;
    policy for advanced economies and,
    140; relocation decisions and, 79-81;
    in São Paulo, 153. *See also* Manu-
    facturing sector
Infrastructure, 36, 84, 138; investment,
    6; middle-income countries and, 46,
    47; in Soviet Union, 157; spatial
    policies and, 130
Innovation: agricultural, 94-95, 148;
    diffusion of, 81-82, 100
Input-output relations, regional planning
    and, 62-64
Investment, 38; demographic projections
    and, 89; economic activity and, 61;
    industrial, 55; infrastructure, 6, 36;

manufacturing, 79; regional, 124-28;
    in Soviet Union, 157; in transport,
    70-71, 72, 73
Iran, 48, 71
Iraq, 48
Israel, 47, 48, 49
Ivory Coast, 29, 105, 137

Jamaica, 29
Japan, 26, 29, 65, 119-21, 126-28

Kenya, 44
Kontuly, Thomas, 112
Korea, 27, 56, 63, 68, 113, 121; employ-
    ment in provinces in, 86 n.29;
    industrial estates in, 82-83; land-
    ownership in, 94-95; trade and, 37-
    38, 46-47
Kuala Lumpur, 56
Kuwait, 29, 31

Labor, 110; location choices and, 84;
    mobility patterns and, 59; transport
    and, 69, 70
Land: city-states and, 42; spatial de-
    velopment and, 36-37; transport and,
    71
Landownership: absentee, 71; in Latin
    America, 147-48; settlement patterns
    and, 93-95
Large low-income countries: typology
    data on, 172-73, 175; urbanization
    strategies and, 43-45, 136-37
Latin America, 45, 119; middle-income
    countries in, 49-50; natural urban
    population increase in, 31; regional
    disparities and, 99; regional policies
    and, 149-51; regions of, 142-46; rural
    landholding in, 93-94; settlement
    policies and, 141, 151-55; spatial
    development in, 146-49; transport
    networks in, 68; transport policies
    and, 141-42; typology data on, 174;
    urbanization levels and, 19. *See also*
    specific Latin American countries
Lebanon, 47
Libya, 47, 48
Limited domestic market countries:
    typology data on, 171-72; urbaniza-
    tion strategies and, 42-43, 133-36
Literacy, 38, 46

Location, 7, 59, 139; in advanced economies, 51; business, 101; constraints on, 83-87; corporations and, 64; manufacturing employment and, 73-75, 83; population concentration and, 42; in provinces, 81-83, 84, 86; relocation decisions and, 79-81; in São Paulo, 153; small cities and, 67; tariffs and problems of, 105; transport and, 68, 73

Madagascar, 71
Malaysia, 46, 56, 93, 125
Manufacturing sector, 62, 126; branch plants and, 81-83; in centrally planned economies, 52; city size and, 65-66; location policies and, 64, 83-87; in middle-income countries, 46, 49; migration and, 88; population concentration and, 73-75; relocation decisions and, 79-81; trade protection and, 103; transport and, 72. *See also* Industry
Market and mixed economies, 39; typology data on, 171-74
Mediterranean countries, 45, 47, 49; typology data on, 173-74
Mera, Koichi, 120
Mexico, 49, 56, 99; regional disparity in, 150-51; settlement patterns in, 141
Mexico City, 56, 105, 113
Middle Eastern countries, 45, 47-49, 119; typology data on, 173-74
Middle-income countries, 6, 10; city classification and, 59; differentiating, 45-46; economic efficiency and, 111-12; new towns and, 113, 114; policy adaptations and, 59, 137, 138; population growth and, 139; procurement policies and, 102 n.3; spatial policies and, 116-17; typology data on, 173-74, 175; urbanization policies and, 45-50, 137-39
Migration, 7, 10, 15, 36, 55, 106, 130, 139, 153; in advanced economies, 50; in centrally planned economies, 52; in China, 159; city-to-city, 59; economic efficiency and, 110, 111-12; erratic changes in, 13; in India, 44; international, 27, 29, 37; in Korea, 94; in Middle Eastern

countries, 48; reducing, 89-91; rural-urban, 29, 30-31, 59; in Soviet Union, 22, 157; transport and, 70; urban growth and, 16, 165-66; urbanization policies and, 87-88
Mills, Edwin S., 37
Minimum wage law, 105-06, 110
Mobility patterns, 11; distribution of income and, 37; employment and, 88; industrial, 80; interurban, 29; labor force, 59; manufacturing and, 75-79; in middle-income countries, 46; of resources, 10, 50, 116, 140; socioeconomic, 123; urban-urban, 112
Morocco, 47
Muda irrigation project (Malaysia), 92-93, 125-26

National Plan for Human Settlements (Mexico), 149
National security, 99-100
New towns: growth-center strategies and, 113-16; inefficiency of, 130-31; problems with, examples of, 161-62; transport and, 73; in United States, 162
New Zealand, 22
Nigeria, 44, 103, 137

Oceania, 22
Output, 64; farm sector and, 9, 92; manufacturing and, 46; regional planning and, 62-64; spatial planning and, 6, 7

Pakistan, 43
Papua New Guinea, 27, 56
Paraguay, 151
People's Republic of China. *See* China
Peru, 49, 142, 150
Philippines, 46
Planners, 96-97, 101
Policies. *See* Procurement policies; Spatial policies; Urbanization policies
Pollution, 110; new towns and, 114; policy and, 137-38
Population: concentration of, 101; data on growth rates and, 167-69; decline,, 140; economic growth and, 65; industrialization and, 73-87; land-ownership and, 94; migration redirection and, 89-91; national spatial de-

velopment and, 36-38; national
urbanization strategies and, 38-53;
optimal size of cities and, 56-57;
policies, 132; projection of, 13-15;
redistribution, 7; in Soviet Union,
156; urban, 12-13; urbanization of,
5-6; urbanization trends and, 13-36
Port Moresby, 56
Portugal, 29, 49
Pred, Alan, 61, 62, 63
Primacy: defining, 107-08; index, 170;
large cities and, 32-36
Private sector, 6, 83
Procurement policies, 102
Projects Counter (São Paulo), 153
Protection. *See* Trade protection
Public sector, 6; investment in Muda
project, 125-26; investment in São
Paulo, 153

Railroads, 69
Regional development, 61; input-output
relations and, 62-63
Regional inequalities, 39, 53, 99; resources and, 130; spatial policy,
dualism, and, 116-28; trade protection and, 102-03
Regional Plan Association of New York,
42
Regional and Urban Development Policy
(PDUR, São Paulo), 153, 155
Regulation (government), policy and,
105-06
Republic of Korea. *See* Korea
Resources: human, 38, 46; mobility
of, 10, 50, 116, 140; reallocation of,
123; water, 37
Road projects, rural, 70-72, 100
Rural sector, 133, 136, 137, 163; bias
against, 104-05, 130; in centrally
planned economies, 52; in China,
158; landownership and, 93-95;
in Latin America, 147-48; in middle-
income countries, 46, 47, 49; national growth and, 121; population
decline and, 27, 29; population increases and, 15, 16-17; population
redistribution and, 12-13; road
projects and, 70-72; urban development interaction and, 91-93; urbanization levels and, 17, 27; urban
policy and, 4, 8, 9-10, 99

São Paulo, 113; settlement patterns
in, 151-55
Saudi Arabia, 29, 48
Seoul, 47, 56, 94
Services, 48, 52, 84; city structure and,
66; distribution among cities of,
61-62; manufacturing employment
and, 73; policy and, 139; in Soviet
Union, 157; transport and, 69
Settlements: centrally planned economies and, 51-53; economic efficiency
and, 110-11; interurban mobility
and, 29; in Latin America, 141, 150,
151-55; in Mexico, 149; patterns of,
7; rural aspect of, 17, 93-95; in
Soviet Union, 158; stop-and-go
policies and, 9; strategies, 6; transport and, 67-73
Singapore, 29, 42, 56, 113; primacy and,
32
Small countries, national urbanization
strategies and, 42
Social capital, 120-21
Song, Byong Nak, 37
Soviet Union: settlement patterns in,
51-53; urbanization in, 156-58;
urbanization levels and, 19, 22
Spain, 49
Spatial development, 36-38
Spatial policies, 3, 4, 5, 11; biases in,
101, 104-05, 129-30; Latin America
and, 146-49, 150; national economic
policy and, 101-07; national policy
and, 98; output and, 6, 7; planners
and, 96-97; regional inequality and,
116-28; social forces and, 85-86;
trade policies and, 8; urbanization
strategies and, 38-53
Stohr, Walter, 150
Sudan, 44, 48
Sweden, 29, 64
Syria, 48

Taiwan, 46, 47, 68, 94
Tanzania, 44, 137
Taxes, 106-07, 110, 131, 153
Technology: branch plants and, 82;
farmers and, 94
Thailand, 46
Tokyo, 113, 128
Tolley, George, 112
Towns. *See* New towns

Trade, 46; spatial development and, 37-38, 49
Trade policies, 8
Trade protection: anti-agricultural bias and, 104; industrial incentives and, 102-04
Transport, 7, 66, 120, 121; corridors, 69-70, 72, 131; decentralization and, 83; migration and, 88; policy and, 99, 130, 139; policy implications and, 72-73; provincial branches and, 86 n.29; rural road projects and, 70-72, 100; tariffs, 105; urban concentration and, 67-69
Tunisia, 47
Turkey, 27, 48

Ulsan (Korea), 63
Unemployment, 81, 84, 101; minimum wage law and, 105-06
Union of Soviet Socialist Republics. *See* Soviet Union
United Kingdom. *See* Great Britain
United States, 5, 59, 65; procurement policies and, 102 n.3; urbanization levels and, 26-27
Urbanization: in Africa, 18-19; in Asia, 19, 46-47; in China, 51-53; comparative data on, 163-75; development policies and, 36-38; in Europe, 22; expanding and mature, 57-59, 140; by geographic region, 17-27; by individual countries, 22-27; large cities and, 31-36; in Latin America, 19, 49-50; level of, 17; in Mediterranean countries, 49; in Middle East, 47-49; national strategies and, 38-53; in Oceania, 22; primacy and, 108; sources of, 16-17; in Soviet Union, 22, 51-53; tempo of, 27-29; worldwide trends of, 12-36
Urbanization policies, 4; advanced economies and, 50-51, 140; basic considerations for, 64-67, 129-31; bias against agriculture and, 104-05; border regions and, 99-100; centrally planned economies and, 51-53; city size and, 56-57; classification of cities and, 59-60; classification of countries and, 39-42; classifying policy measures and, 131-33; constraints on, 36-38; economic integration and,

56; expanding or mature urbanization and, 57-59; failure of, 9; fiscal policy and, 106-07; formulation of appropriate, 7-10; government regulations and, 105-06; importance of, 5-7; industrialization, population, and, 73-87; large low-income countries and, 43-45, 137-39; in Latin America, 144-55; limited domestic markets and, 42-43, 133-36; location choice constraints and, 83-87; middle-income countries and, 45-50, 137-39; migration of labor and, 87-91; objectives of, 7, 9, 97, 98-101, 150; peripheral regions and, 99; personal relations and, 85-86; planning and, 96-97; political integration and, 100; primacy and, 32; regional inequalities and, 39, 53, 99, 116-28; rural landholdings and, 93-95; rural-urban interaction and, 91-93; size, location, and function of cities and, 59-60; small countries and, 42; timing and, 98; trade and, 102-04; transport and, 67-73; unintended spatial effects and, 101-07; urban concentration and, 107-16; weakness of, 96-98
Urban sector, 133, 136, 137, 163; in Africa, 45; in Asia, 43-44; in centrally planned economies, 51, 52; landownership and, 94; in Latin American countries, 49, 147-48; in Middle Eastern countries, 48; population increases and, 15-16; population redistribution and, 12-13; primacy and, 32-36, 107-08; rural development interaction and, 91-93; rural growth differential and, 27-29; in São Paulo, 153, 155
Uruguay, 29, 49-50, 142, 150

Venezuela, 29, 49, 142, 146
Vining, Daniel R., 112

Wages. *See* Minimum wage law
Water resources, 37; Middle Eastern countries and, 49
Williamson, Jeffrey, 117, 118

Yemen, 48

Zaire, 44

The full range of World Bank publications, both free and for sale, is described in the *Catalog of World Bank Publications*; the continuing research program is outlined in *World Bank Research Program: Abstracts of Current Studies*. Both booklets are updated annually; the most recent edition of each is available without charge from the Publications Unit, World Bank, 1818 H Street, N.W., Washington, D.C. 20433, U.S.A.

Bertrand Renaud is chief of the Urban Affairs Division of the Organisation for Economic Co-operation and Development. He was formerly an economist with the Development Policy Staff of the World Bank.